Card Game Roundup

Math Games that Roam the Concept Range

by Trudy Bortz
and Josh Rappaport

Card Game Roundup

Math Games that Roam the Concept Range

Published by:
Singing Turtle Press
#770, 3530 Zafarano Drive #6
Santa Fe, NM 87507

Tel: 1/505-438-3418
Fax: 1/505-438-7742
www.SingingTurtle.com
E-mail: kyle@SingingTurtle.com

Text copyright 2002, by Singing Turtle Press
Illustrations copyright 2002, by Sally Blakemore
Cover design by Sally Blakemore and David Cox
All rights reserved.
First printing 2002
ISBN: 0-9659113-9-X

The publisher expresses appreciation to Clair Schoolmaster, Jennifer Kadlubek and Toni Burger,
who tested many of these games in their classrooms and provided invaluable feedback.
The publisher also thanks Ari and Ella Rappaport, who helped develop these games and offered many suggestions.

— Attention Teachers / Administrators —
For information on volume discounts to schools, visit us at: SingingTurtle.com
Or call us at the phone number above.

Contents

Introduction

We wrote this book because we have had fun and success using card games to teach math concepts, and we want to share some of our games with you.

The games in this book have evolved through years of practice in both the classroom setting and the tutoring office (Trudy is a teacher, Josh a tutor). Because of that, they may be used by classroom teachers, private tutors, parents of schooled children for enrichment, and parents of homeschooled children as part of the curriculum.

Cards are a great learning tool for youngsters. Children know that cards are part of "grown-up" play, so they view cards as exciting and sophisticated. Not only that, but cards have a variety of attributes (number, suit and color) which can be used to let children explore not only number operations, but also patterning, data analysis, probability and geometry.

The game rules as presented are those that have worked best for us. But feel free to modify rules — or create new games and extensions — as suits the needs of the children you work with.

Some children will have never used playing cards before. To introduce these children to the number aspects of cards, we provide the first game, Racing Rattlers. To introduce these children to the suit aspects of cards, we provide the second game, "Hungry" Hank. The remaining games cover a range of math competencies: number operations, patterning, geometry, data analysis, and probability.

Many games come with reproducible gameboards, and you will find these gameboards following the rules for those games. We also provide two general-use worksheets that children can use to help them do addition in many of the games. Worksheet A on p.94 provides an organized space to let children add two numbers; Worksheet B on p.95 is for adding three or more numbers.

When choosing a game, consider the skill the game is designed to teach, the ability level of the children, size of group, and the amount of adult supervision available. Children often need to see new games modeled several times, but once they master the rules, they can play independently. Younger children may need to play in a small group with an adult to understand the concepts and to develop strategies for basic number operations.

Most of these games can be played in large groups, small groups, or individually. It often helps to teach the games to a large group using overhead projector cards and making transparencies of the necessary gameboards. Then let children play the games in small groups.

You can also choose whether children play the coooperative or competitive version of the game. Depending on your classroom routines and children's temperaments, both cooperative and competitive games can be effective learning tools. Adding competition often adds excitement and increased motivation for children to gain and/or practice skills.

We hope you enjoy using these card games. Happy trails!

How to Use the Ikons

**Card Game Roundup uses ikons to guide you through the games.
Here's a view of the ikons and a description of how they can help you.**

STORYLINE, in the upper-left corner of each game's opening page, provides a story that grounds the game in a Wild West theme.

We suggest that the Educator read the **STORYLINE** aloud to children, for the more they connect with the story, the more engaged they will be in playing the game.

CONCEPT CORRAL, located just below **STORYLINE**, details the NCTM standards involved in each game: Number & Operation, Geometry, Problem Solving, Connections, etc. Each subsection of the **CORRAL** offers details on how the game meets the standard.

Use **CONCEPT CORRAL** to document how using the book helps you meet the math standards and competencies in your area.

Note that a chart on p.96 conveniently displays the NCTM standards involved in each of the 18 games.

CAMPFIRE CHAT

CAMPFIRE CHAT offers follow-up questions and activities that help you bring out the rich mathematical content in the games

CAMPFIRE CHAT offers a variety of questions: some close-ended, others open-ended. Answers are offered, when appropriate. Since every game has **CAMPFIRE CHAT** questions, every game addresses NCTM's communications standard.

TIPS AND POINTERS

TIPS and POINTERS, in the black box after **CAMPFIRE CHAT**, offers time-tested advice for each game.

Read through the **TIPS and POINTERS** before playing to develop strategies that make optimal use of each game.

ROUNDUP

ROUNDUP does just what you'd expect ... tells you the supplies to rustle up before children can play.

Most supplies are readily at hand, and the book provides the reproducible worksheets and gamesheets you need.

ROUNDUP is found in the margin on the right-hand page of every game spread.

5

Relaxing on their day off, cowhands make pretend rattlesnakes out of cards. And they compete to see who can make their rattler most quickly. By playing this game, children get an introduction to the suits and numbers of cards, and at the same time, learn a thing or two about ascending and descending order.

CONCEPT CORRAL

NUMBER & OPERATION
➤ Count, recognize, and order numbers.

ALGEBRA
➤ Identify and classify cards by suit and by magnitude of number.

REASONING
➤ Distinguish between ascending and descending order.

REPRESENTATION
➤ Arrange a string of numbers in ascending and descending order.

Racing Rattlers

GAME A
Cooperative/Competitive

GOAL: To make rattlers using ascending order.

 # Players: 1, 2, 3, or 4. With four players, each child can pick a suit.

NOTE: See Tips & Pointers 4 for distinction between competitive and cooperative play.

1 Shuffle cards and place deck face down. Lay all aces face up one next to the other. (See Diagram A on p.8.)

2 Each child takes a turn drawing a card from deck and turning it face up.

3 If card turned over is a 2, it may be placed above ace of the same suit. i.e. If child turns over 2 of spades, he places it above ace of spades. A child may at first lay down only a 2 of any suit. After laying down a 2 of a certain suit, he may lay down a 3 of that same suit. If a card comes up that may not be used, it is placed in a discard pile.

4 A child may take top card off discard pile instead of off deck.

5 As one example of a game, cards might be laid down in an order like this: 2 of spades, 2 of clubs, 2 of hearts, 3 of clubs, 3 of hearts, 2 of diamonds, 4 of clubs ... etc.

6 After all cards in deck have been played, shuffle discard pile and resume play.

7 Game ends when all four snakes are complete (in cooperative play), or when the first snake gets completed (in competitive play).

GAME B
Cooperative/Competitive

GOAL: To make rattlers using descending order.

 # Players: 1, 2, 3, or 4.

Same rules as in Game A, except that now instead of laying down all four aces, children first lay down all four 10s. Subsequent cards are laid down in descending order: 10, 9, 8, ... etc. (See Diagram B on p.8.)

GAME C
Cooperative/Competitive

GOAL: To make rattlers using both ascending and descending order.

 # Players: 1, 2, 3, or 4.

Same rules as in Game A and Game B, except that now instead of laying down just aces or just 10s, children lay down both aces and 10s. On any turn, children may use a card that ascends or descends. i.e. On first turn, a child could lay down a 2 (ascending order) or a 9 (descending order). (See Diagram C on p.8.)

1 Which cards can possibly be laid down on the first turn in either Game A or Game B? **A: Four cards can be laid down at the start of these games: the four 2s in Game A; the four 9s in Game B.**

2 Which cards can possibly be laid down on the first turn in Game C? **A: Eight cards: the four 2s and the four 9s.**

3 Which games allow you to build the snake faster: the games allowing just ascending or descending order, or the game allowing both ascending and descending order? **A: Game C, which allows both ascending and descending order, for in this game you get twice as many opportunities to lay down cards.**

4 Why does the snake get built slowly at first, but faster and faster as the game progresses? **A: When the game begins, the deck is large, and only a few cards can be laid down. So you have to go through a lot of cards you cannot use to find the few you can use. As the game continues, the deck gets smaller and smaller, so you don't have to go through as many cards to find the cards you need.**

5 Did it ever happen that a snake got stuck and no new cards could be added to it? Can you explain how this happens? **A: If a card that you need next is buried in the discard pile, the snake will be unable to grow until the disard pile is shuffled and play resumes.**

6 Is this a game of skill, or a game of chance? **A: This is purely a game of chance. The way you can tell is that children make no decisions as they play, except the decision of which suit to root for in the competitive versions — and that isn't a decision involving skill.**

ROUNDUP

FOR EACH CHILD OR GROUP OF CHILDREN:

➤ One deck with all picture cards and Jokers removed. The ace stands for the number 1.

➤ Racing Rattlers Card Layout master on p.8, to give children a sense of what the layouts look like.

➤ A big open space where children can spread out their cards.

TIPS AND POINTERS

1 This is a good beginner's game for working on number recognition and sequencing numbers from 1-10.

2 Tell children they will be making a number snake either on the floor or on a tabletop.

3 It helps to model the entire process of laying down cards before children play. When you do this, point out that cards must be laid down by suit. In other words, a spade must be laid on top of another spade, a heart on top of a heart, etc.

4 Difference between competitive and cooperative play is largely a difference in attitude. In both competitive and cooperative play, children lay down cards for all four snakes. But in the competitive games, children root for a suit of their choice. One other difference: in cooperative games, play ends when all snakes have been created; in competitive games, play ends when the first snake gets completed, for at that point one child has won.

Racing Rattlers
Card Layout Master

Diagram A (Game A)

Diagram B (Game B)

Diagram C (Game C)

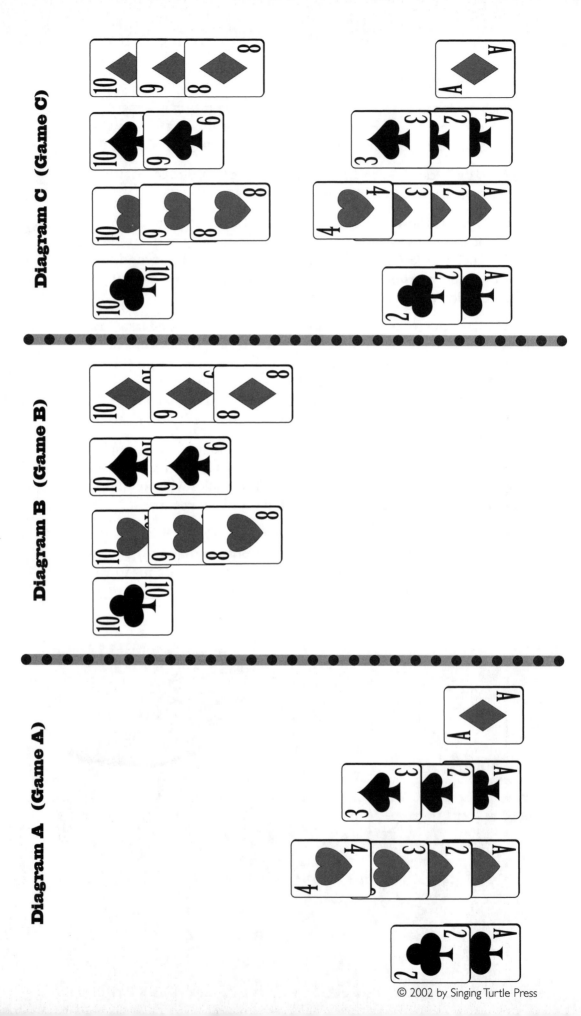

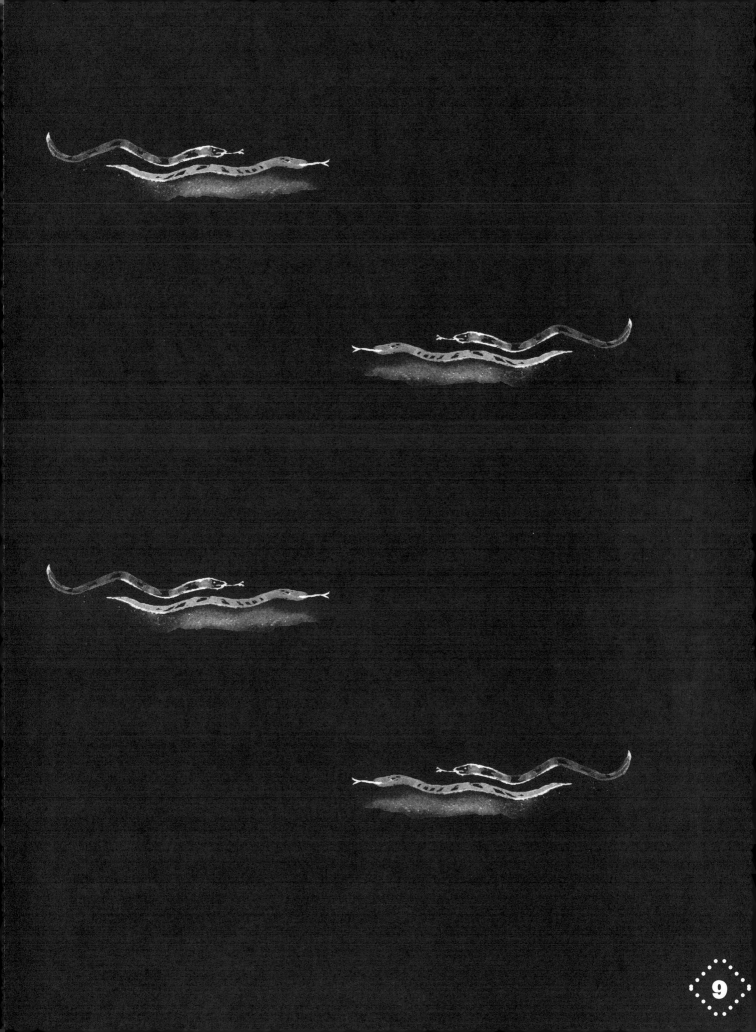

STORYLINE

Hank the ranchhand has spent all day rustling cattle. Now he wants some food. But other cowpokes are hungry too, and he needs to hurry to the Cook's Pot before they beat him to the food. Can Hank get to the Cook's Pot in time? If children play their cards right, Hank just might get a nice hot supper. And if not that, at least cold leftovers.

CONCEPT CORRAL

ALGEBRA & PATTERNS

➤ Recognize and name numbers.

➤ Recognize and name suits.

➤ Group cards by suit and number.

REASONING

➤ Figure out what assortment of cards helps Hank get his meal, and what assortment makes it hard for him to get his meal.

➤ Figure out what arrangment of cards either helps or hurts Hank in his attempt to get a meal.

"Hungry" Hank

GAME A Cooperative

GOAL: To help Hank get to the Cook's Pot before the other cowpokes eat up all the supper. Cowpokes do this by getting five cards in a row.

 # Players: 1, 2, 3, or 4.

1 Children take one copy of the Cook's Pot from the master on p.13 and place it one foot away from themselves. Children make one deck of 10 cards as described in the Roundup. They place deck face down, then say, "Hungry-Hungry-Hank!" On the word "Hank!" they turn the first card over, and lay it face up so that it is pointing toward the Cook's Pot. (See Sample Game on p.13.)

2 Children again say, "Hungry-Hungry-Hank!", and on "Hank!" turn over the second card. Then they figure out whether or not second card helps Hank get his meal. The card may be put in a line toward Cook's Pot only if its suit or number matches that of the first card. i.e. If first card is 3 of hearts, only a 3 or a heart may be placed on top of it.

3a If second card does match first card in number or suit, children place it on top of first card and heading toward Cook's Pot (see Sample Game on p.13) and draw another card.

3b If second card does not match first card in number or suit, children discard it and draw another card.

4 Children need to get five cards in a row for Hank to get his food. If they get five in a row before running out of their 10 cards, Hank gets supper. If they run out of cards before they get five cards, then Hank does not get supper and therefore earns his unfortunate nickname.

Extension: If children cannot get Hank to the Cook's Pot in time, they can look at all 10 of their cards and try to arrange any five of them so Hank does get food. In this case, they say that Hank didn't get warm food, but at least he got cold leftovers.

Follow-Up Play: Whether or not children get Hank to the Cook's Pot in time, they re-shuffle deck and try again. It's interesting for children to try five times with the same deck and keep track of how many times Hank gets his meal. Then they can switch to another deck and keep track of their success with that deck. This can lead them to ponder why one deck might lead Hank to more success than another deck.

GOAL: To be the first buckaroo to the Cook's Pot by being the first to get five cards in a row. Whoever is first gets the best helping of food.

 # Players: 2, 3, or 4. With 4, it's fun to play pair vs. pair.

1 Each player gets her own deck of 10 cards (the same kind of random decks used in Game A) and lays it face down. Players are positioned so that they all face the Cook's Pot. One arrangement that works well is to place the Cook's Pot in center of table or floor and have all players sit around it.

2 Players say, "Hungry-Hungry-Hank!" and on the word "Hank!" each player turns over her first card, and sets it up about a foot away from the Cook's Pot but pointing toward the Cook's Pot.

3 Players again say: "Hungry-Hungry-Hank!" and turn over their second card. Players check to see if the second card can be placed on top of the first card by matching it in number or suit. Those who can place second card on top do so; those who cannot discard that card.

4 Play continues until one player gets five cards in a row and places the fifth card on the Cook's Pot. This player wins, for she is the first one to get to the Cook's Pot, and she therefore gets the best supper. Of course, it is possible that two or more children reach the Cook's Pot at the same time. In this case, they tie.

Extension: If no children bring Hank to the Cook's Pot before they run out of cards, each child can look at all 10 of their cards and try to arrange any five of them so Hank does get to the Cook's Pot. In this case, they say that Hank didn't get warm food, but at least he got cold leftovers.

Follow-Up Play: As in Game A, children can re-shuffle their decks and play again. After a while, it's a good idea to have them switch decks — round-robin fashion — and see if they have better luck with a different deck. Again this can promote discussion about why one deck might lead Hank to more success than another deck. Educators may have each group choose its favorite deck and talk about why it is such a good deck for Hank.

CAMPFIRE CHAT

1 Does the order of the cards in your deck ever make a difference in this game? **A: The order can make a big difference. Children can notice this through situations in which they can't reach the Cook's Pot with the original order their deck's cards are in, but they can reach it if they re-order the cards.**

2 Is it possible for Hank to get to the Cook's Pot with just five cards? If so, can you put five cards together so that Hank can get to the Cook's Pot with those five cards? **A: Yes, it is possible, and this exercise gives children**

ROUNDUP

FOR EACH GROUP OF CHILDREN:

➳ **One copy of the Cook's Pot from the master on p.13.**

➳ **One copy of the Sample Game from the master on p.13.**

➳ **Game A: Take a deck and remove all picture cards and Jokers. Shuffle deck and split it into four piles of 10 cards. Each pile of 10 cards is a deck for this game. Note that you end up with four decks (each different from the other), and the group of children can try different decks to see if they give Hank a better or worse chance to get his meal.**

➳ **Game B: Now each child playing uses one of the four decks created in Game A, as described above.**

a chance to further their understanding of the matching aspects of this game.

3 When you get a card you can use, what is more often true? That it matches the suit of the card before it, or that it matches the number of the card before it? **A: Cards match in suit more than in number. That's because any given card has nine other cards with the same suit but only three other cards with the same number. e.g. If card is 3 of hearts, there are nine other hearts, but only three other 3s.**

4 What kind of deck makes it easy for Hank to get to the Cook's Pot? **A: A deck with a lot of cards of the same suit or a lot of cards of the same number.**

5 What kind of deck makes it hard for Hank to get to the Cook's Pot? **A: A deck with few cards of the same suit and few or no cards of the same number.**

6 Can you make a deck in which Hank is sure to get his meal, no matter what order the cards are in? **A: This is possible. One way — make a deck in which all cards share the same suit. e.g. A deck made of all hearts: ace of hearts through 10 of hearts.**

7 Can you make a deck in which Hank will never get to the Cook's Pot, no matter how the cards are arranged. **A: This too is possible. One such deck has one card of each number (ace through 10) and no more than four cards of the same suit. Example: Ace of hearts / 2 of hearts / 3 of hearts / 4 of hearts / 5 of spades / 6 of spades / 7 of spades / 8 of spades / 9 of clubs / 10 of clubs. Let children try a deck like this. Then see if they can make a deck of their own that gives Hank no chance to get his meal.**

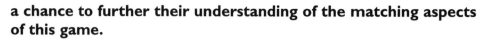

TIPS AND POINTERS

1 This game can be used to teach children unfamiliar with cards the numbers and suits.

2 If Educator has children play the game more than once, she may want to vary the name to "Hungry Henrietta" or "Hungry Harriet".

3 Another fun follow-up game for Game A or Game B: Allow children to look at all 10 of their cards. Then challenge them to see how long a chain they can make with those 10 cards. In other words, they need to arrange their cards in such a way that from one card to the next either the suit or the number is the same, and they try to see how many cards they can put in a row. In many cases, children will be able to put all 10 cards in a line.

"Hungry" Hank
Sample Game

STORYLINE

Preparing to compete at the upcoming rodeo, young cowhands test their skill at hitting a target. To perfect their skill, they figure out their rate of success at various distances. In the process, they get a fun, hands-on lesson in measurement and data analysis.

CONCEPT CORRAL

MEASUREMENT
➤ Compare lengths of distances using a nonstandard unit (a cut-out paper horseshoe).

DATA ANALYSIS & PROBABILITY
➤ Discover patterns in data, and analyze how throwing from various distances affects children's rate of success in hitting a target.

REASONING
➤ Develop hypotheses to account for the data.

CONNECTIONS
➤ Find connections between measurement and data analysis.

REPRESENTATION
➤ Record hits and misses on a chart. Then use that information to fill in a bar graph.

Annie Oakley

GAME A
Cooperative

GOAL: To throw an object into a bucket from a distance determined by a chance draw of a card. Next, to record the result of each throw. Then to represent the data on a bar graph. Finally, to look for patterns in the data.

 # Players: 1, 2, 3, or 4.

1 Shuffle deck and place face down. On each turn, a child draws top card. Number on card tells child how many horseshoes (copied off master on p.18) to take.

2 Child places that many horseshoes in a line starting at the target (trash barrel or bucket).

3 Standing just behind the last horseshoe, child tries to throw object into basket or at target.

4 If he hits target, he marks chart with smiley face; if he misses, he marks the chart with sad face.

5 Game continues until children draw all 40 cards and make 40 tosses or rolls. (If you prefer a shorter game, take out a suit or two and use just 30 or 20 cards and throws. But don't use just 10; not enough data for a meaningful analysis!)

6 After children record throws on Data Sheet, they fill out Annie Oakley Bar Graph by coloring up to correct number for each distance. In other words, if they got 2 shots in from the distance of 4, they color the bar up to 2 at the 4 distance. Make sure children understand that if they got no hits at a certain distance, the bar for that distance remains uncolored.

Follow-Up Activity: Educator holds up one group's bar graph and ask a child from another group if he can read and interpret the bar graph. Children from group whose data is used give feedback as to whether or not child interprets data correctly.

CAMPFIRE CHAT

1 Looking at your data sheet and graph, what do you notice about your group's success in hitting the target as you stood farther from it? **A: Children should see that they hit target less frequently the farther away from it they stand.**

2 If you see a pattern, how does it show up on the Data Sheet? How does it show up on the Bar Graph? **A: Data Sheet shows fewer hits at the top, more hits at the bottom. Bar Graph descends in an overall way from left to right.**

3 If you see a pattern, why do you think it's there? **A: Greater distance from target makes it harder to hit the target.**

4 In this activity, the success in hitting the target went down as the distance from the target went up. Can you think of other situations or activities in which one factor goes down as another goes up? (i.e. The less you eat all day, the hungrier you are at end of day; if you want to get to your friend's house in less time, the more quickly you need to run there; you're less likely to catch a baseball the higher into the air it is thrown; etc.) **A: Answers will vary.**

TIPS AND POINTERS

1 You will need to run off and cut out many horseshoes. Laminating horseshoes ensures they'll last for years. Or you can use another manipulative measuring tool in your classroom such as blocks, rulers, etc. But make sure any manipulative used is at least 10" long. Otherwise it's so easy for children to make shots that they won't get enough misses to create a broad data spread.

2 Show children how to line up horseshoes end-to-end, discussing what happens to measurement's accuracy if children line horseshoes up carelessly.

3 Show children how to record on Annie Oakley Data Sheet. You may want to model recording the first few results for one team to get everyone started.

4 Once children fill in Data Sheet, show them how to fill in Annie Oakley Bar Graph.

5 You can alter game to make it more or less active / noisy depending on your tolerance. If game gets too loud or noisy, have children use smaller horseshoes and smaller target (a can or some other small container) and let them play game on a table.

6 If children have trouble throwing ball into bucket, you may have them roll it to hit bucket.

ROUNDUP

FOR EACH TEAM OR GROUP:

➤ One deck of the 40 numbered cards (ace through 10), but no picture cards or Jokers.

➤ One Annie Oakley Data Sheet on p. 16, one Annie Oakley Bar Graph on p. 17, and 10 horseshoes copied off the Horseshoe Master on p. 18.

➤ One empty wastebasket or bucket.

➤ One bean bag, sponge ball, or any item children can toss.

Annie Oakley Data Sheet

Mark hits by drawing a smile on the face.
Mark misses by drawing a frown on the face.

Card Drawn	Throw #1	Throw #2	Throw #3	Throw #4	Total # Hits
10					
9					
8					
7					
6					
5					
4					
3					
2					
1					

Annie Oakley Bar Graph

Color space between bars to show number of hits at each distance.

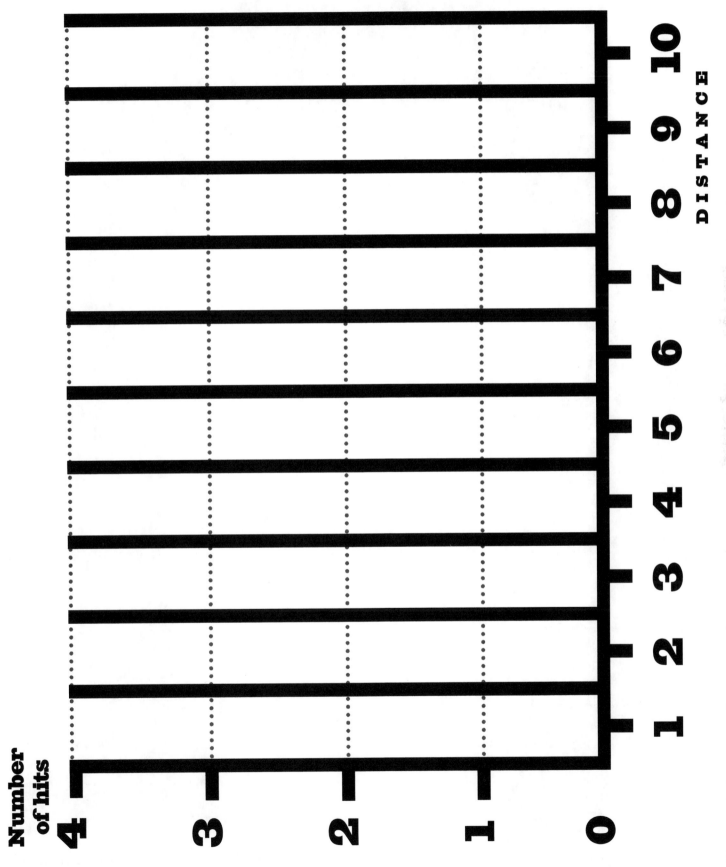

Annie Oakley Horseshoe Master

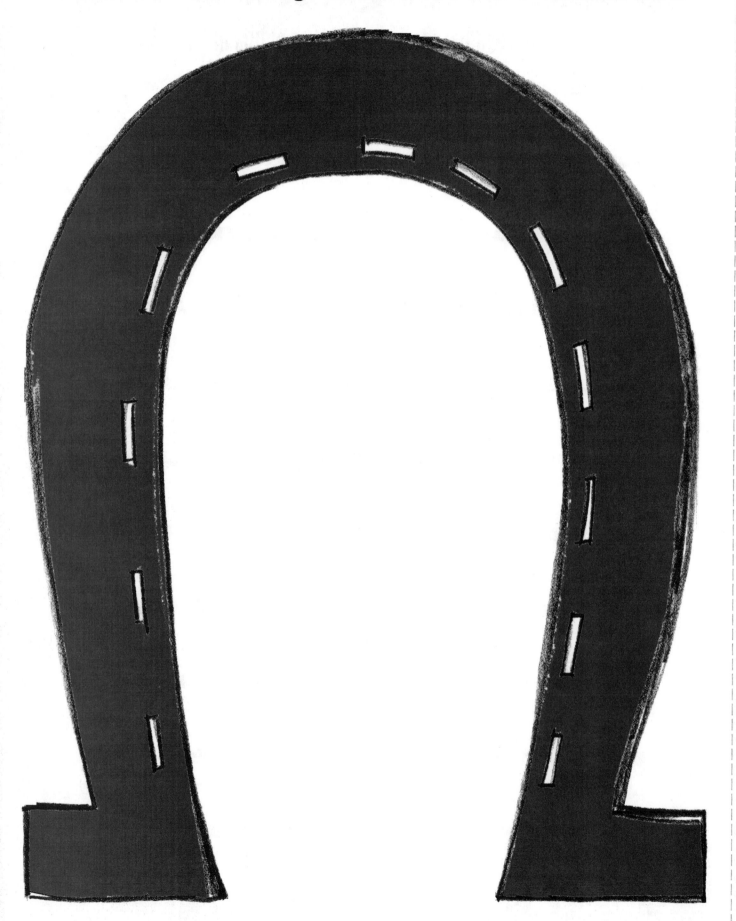

HISTORY CONNECTION
The Story of Annie Oakley

Annie Oakley is the most famous markswoman in American history.

By the age of 12, she could shoot the head off a running quail. But it wasn't until she beat a famous marksman, Frank Butler, in a contest in 1875 that the world took notice of this young lady's remarkable skill with a gun.

Annie was so talented that she became a featured performer in Buffalo Bill's "Wild West Show". During the show Annie, known as "Little Sure Shot," performed amazing shots from a distance of 30 paces, including:

➤ Shooting a dime tossed in the air,

➤ Shooting a hole in a playing card,

➤ Shooting the tip off a cigarette when it was perched in the lips of a certain daring gentleman. (The gentleman, it turns out, was usually Annie's husband, Mr. Butler, who became her agent after she beat him in the shooting contest.)

To this day the name Annie Oakley stands for excellence and accuracy, traits important in mathematics as well as in marksmanship!

STORYLINE

At a square dance, cowboys and cowgirls get a fun lesson in odd and even. They discover that they can tell if a number is odd or even by getting that number of dancers on the floor, then seeing whether or not every dancer has a partner.

CONCEPT CORRAL

NUMBER & OPERATION

➤ Use a multi-sensory activity to figure out if a number is odd or even.

➤ Create visualizations to figure out if a number is odd or even.

ALGEBRA

➤ Search for patterns in odd and even numbers.

REASONING

➤ Test a hunch about odd and even numbers.

CONNECTIONS

➤ Associate a geometric property of a number with the attribute of odd or even.

REPRESENTATION

➤ Represent odd or even numbers using manipulatives.

"Howdy Do!"

GAME A
Cooperative

GOAL: To learn about odd and even numbers by playing a dance game.

 # Players: 11 or more.

1 One child picks a card from the deck, announces the number on card to the group, then that number of children get up and form a line. Tell children that this is a dance, and that every child seeks a partner. Encourage children to dance as they get up and move around. Western music puts children even more in the mood to do so. When they meet their partner, they say, "Howdy Do!"

2 First and second child in line greet each other and move so that they stand across from each other. Same for third and fourth children, fifth and sixth, etc. Explain that if every child in line ends up with a partner, the number chosen is even; if one child does not have a partner, the number is odd.

3 As children figure out if each number is odd or even, one child writes the results on the "Howdy Do!" Worksheet on p.23. Or a teacher can write this on the blackboard or on an overhead.

4 If the number is odd, the child who did not get a partner gets to pick and announce the card for the next set of children.

5 Play continues until children have figured out whether or not all the numbers from 1 - 10 are odd or even.

6 Teacher may ask the whole class to answer together or call on individual children.

GAME B
Cooperative

GOAL: To learn about odd and even numbers by playing a game.

 # Players: 2, 3, or 4.

Same concept as Game A, only now children work at desks or tables. After picking out a card, they line up that many counting manipulatives. They try to make two lines so that each manipulative has a partner. If each manipulative has a partner, number is even; if one manipulative does not have a partner, number is odd. Again children record results on the "Howdy Do!" Worksheet on p.23.

 **GAME C**
Cooperative

GOAL: To learn about odd and even numbers by playing a game.

 # Players: 2, 3, or 4.

Play this game after children have had ample practice with Games A and B. Children work in pairs or small groups. One child turns over a card, and announces number on card to all. Children try to figure out mentally whether the number is odd or even, and they record answers on the "Howdy Do!" Worksheet. Children can self-check their answers by using manipulatives. Children compare their answers and resolve any differences.

 **CAMPFIRE CHAT**

1 Once children get a knack for Game A or Game B, ask if they can tell before the pair-up game whether or not a number is odd or even. Ask how they know. **A: Some children will say they can pair up the number of objects in their imagination. Other children will have different strategies. See how many different strategies your children can generate.**

2 When children play Game C, it's great to ask what images they see in their minds — or what strategies they use — to tell whether a number is odd or even. See how many different mental images or strategies your children can describe. **A: Answers will vary.**

3 After children fill out the worksheet in Game C, ask them if they see any pattern in their responses. If children can't find any pattern, suggest that they color all of their odd answers using one color and all of their even answers with another color. The pattern should "jump out" at them. **A: The pattern can be described in various ways. Children often describe it by saying that an even always comes after an odd, and an odd always comes after an even.**

4 Ask children if they can explain why that pattern exists. Perhaps have them demonstrate using a line-up of children or of counting manipulatives. **A: Children should see that if they start with an even number of objects and add one more object, the object added will lack a partner. And then, if they add one more object, the new object can partner up with the previously partnerless object, so the new number of objects will be even.**

ROUNDUP

FOR EACH GROUP OF CHILDREN:

➤ A large clear space for Game A.

➤ One deck with all picture cards and Jokers removed. The ace stands for 1.

➤ "Howdy Do!" Worksheet on p.23.

➤ Manipulative counters (beans, pebbles, buttons, etc.) for Games B and C.

➤ OPTIONAL & FUN: Western music that the children can dance to in Game A.

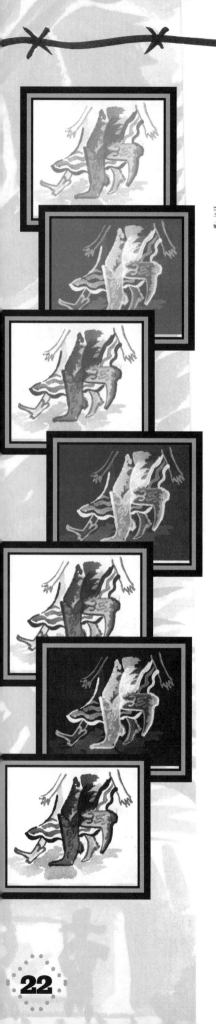

Extension: After children see the alternating pattern for odd and even numbers, ask them if that pattern will hold for the numbers for 11 to 20. Let them test their hunch. If they gain faith in their hunch, see if they can prove it and explain their reasoning. **A: Approaches will vary.**

TIPS AND POINTERS

1 In Game A, use strategies to ensure that the same child won't always be without a partner. Best way to do this is to vary procedure by which children line up and pair up. One procedure is stated in rules. Other procedures include: **a)** having children pair up every other child, **b)** first and last pair up, then next to first and next to last, **c)** having children line up by height and then pairing up. As long as you keep procedures unpredictable, all children will be included.

2 For Game A, it's fun to play square-dance music when dancers take the floor and partner up, then stop the music once children figure out if number is odd or even. You may want to keep music playing quietly during Games B and C as well.

"Howdy Do!" Worksheet

Make a check mark in the correct column to show if the number is odd or even —
or rewrite the number in the correct column to show whether it's odd or even.
You may want to use one color for odd and another color for even.

CARD YOU PICK	ODD	EVEN
1 (Ace)		
2		
3		
4		
5		
6		
7		
8		
9		
10		

Cowpokes meet at noon to "duel" with numbers. They draw from an arsenal of cards and try to lay down either the highest card ... or the lowest. Or the highest or lowest sum. May the good guys win!

CONCEPT CORRAL

NUMBER & OPERATION

➤ Recognize and name numbers.

➤ Order numbers from least to greatest.

DATA ANALYSIS

➤ Figure out how many ways certain numbers can be made with two addends. (See Campfire Chat Questions 4 and 5.)

REASONING

➤ Think through answers to Campfire Chat questions.

CONNECTIONS

➤ Make connections between addition and data by studying the various combinations of addends that can total to a given number.

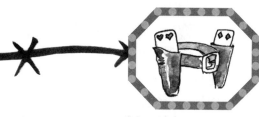

"One-Two-Three-Draw!"

GAME A
Competitive

GOAL: To win card "duels" by playing the highest (or lowest) card.

 # Players: 2, 3, or 4. With 4, it's fun to play pair vs. pair.

Note: This game is like "War" with these differences: **a)** children use number cards only (no picture cards), **b)** there's an element of choice, for children get to choose which of three cards they will use on any given round, **c)** children run through the deck once only in every game.

1 Dealer gives every player (or pair, if playing pairs) three cards, and the players keep these cards hidden from other players.

2 Every player chooses one card to be turned over and stands it up on the table so that no other players may see it. Players say: "One-Two-Three-Draw!" and they lay their cards down on the word "Draw!"

3a Whoever has laid down highest card takes all cards played.

3b If there is a tie for highest number, children who tied play another card from their hand. If they tie on all three cards, Dealer gives each child one card off top of deck to break the tie. Whoever wins the tie takes all cards played.

4 After each round, Dealer gives each child enough cards so that every child starts next round with three cards.

5 When deck runs out, children count cards they have won, and whoever has won the most cards wins that round.

Variation: Same rules except children win by laying down the lowest card.

GOAL: To win card "duels" by playing the highest (or lowest) sums of two cards.

 # Players: 2, 3, or 4. With 4, it's fun to play pair vs. pair.

1 Dealer gives each player (or pair, if playing pairs) three cards, and players keep these cards hidden from other players.

2 Every player chooses two cards to be added together and laid down. Players stand these cards up on the table so that other players cannot see them. Players say: "One-Two-Three-Draw!" and lay down their two chosen cards down on the word "Draw!"

3a Children add up the two cards in every pair laid down. Whichever player lays down the pair with the highest sum wins all cards played in that round.

3b If there is a tie for the highest sum, children who tied play their third card. If this results in another tie, Dealer gives each of the tieing children one card, and children compare those cards. Whoever's card is highest wins and takes all cards played in the round.

4 After each round, Dealer gives every child enough cards so that everyone begins next round with three cards (unless there was a tie, Dealer gives everyone two cards).

5 When deck runs out, children count the cards they have won, and whoever has won the most wins that round.

Variation: Same rules as in Game B, except that now children win by laying down the lowest pair of cards.

1 Are these games based more on skill or on luck? **A: The games are based mostly on luck. You need luck to get dealt the higher (or lower) cards.**

2 What is the highest sum you can make with two cards? **A: 10 (two 5s). Answers will vary if you have added cards to the deck beyond 5s.**

3 What is the lowest sum you can make with two cards? **A: 2 (two aces).**

4 Does this game show you that there are various ways to make a certain sum? In other words, is there only one way to make six with two cards, or are there several ways? Explain. **A: The game shows that there are several pairs of addends that equal certain numbers. For example,**

ROUNDUP

FOR EACH GROUP OF CHILDREN:

➡ **Game A:** Deck with picture cards and Jokers removed. Ace stands for the number 1.

➡ **Game B:** Same deck as in Game A, but remove all cards from 6 through 10.

➡ **OPTIONAL:** "One-Two-Three-Draw!" Card Layout master on p.27 to help children see how game is played.

➡ For children who have trouble holding 3 cards in their hands, use a card holder to help them to see their cards. (See p.93 for directions on making a simple card holder.)

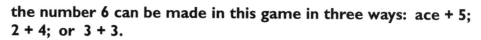

the number 6 can be made in this game in three ways: ace + 5; 2 + 4; or 3 + 3.

5 In how many unique ways can each of the numbers from 2 to 10 be made using two cards from a deck of aces through 5s?

A:

2 (one way: ace + ace)

3 (one way: ace + 2)

4 (two ways: ace + 3; 2 + 2)

5 (two ways: ace + 4; 2 + 3)

6 (three ways: ace + 5; 2 + 4; 3 + 3)

7 (two ways: 2 + 5; 3 + 4)

8 (two ways: 3 + 5; 4 + 4)

9 (one way: 4 + 5)

10 (one way: 5 + 5)

TIPS AND POINTERS

1 If children play pair vs. pair, stress that both children in a pair must agree before they lay down the card or cards. You may also suggest that children take turns holding the cards, for sometimes whoever holds the cards decides what to lay down.

2 Once children become adept adding up to 10 in Game B, you may want to gradually add cards to the deck to encourage them to add to sums greater than 10. Just by including the 6s, for example, children learn to add sums to 12.

3 If you wish children to have a longer game, combine cards from two decks.

4 If Educator does not want children to use the word "Draw!" in this game, a simple alternative is to say: "One-Two-Three-Go!"

"One-Two-Three-Draw!"
Card Layout Master

Game A: High Card Wins

 vs.  |  wins

Game A Variation: Low Card Wins

 vs.  |  wins

Game B: High Pair Wins

 vs.  |  wins

Game B Variation: Low Pair Wins

 vs.  |  wins

Tail-Eating Snakes

CONCEPT CORRAL

NUMBER & OPERATION

➤ Classify polygons by the number of sides they have.

GEOMETRY

➤ Create polygons.

➤ Gain an introduction to concepts of concave and convex polygons.

REASONING

➤ Distinguish polygons from non-polygon shapes.

➤ Distinguish convex polygons from concave polygons.

REPRESENTATION

➤ Make various kinds of polygons using rubber bands and a geoboard.

GAME A Cooperative

GOAL: To create a polygon with any number of sides from three to eight.

 # Players: 1, 2, 3, or 4. Children can play this game individually or in cooperative pairs or groups.

We'll refer to each child or group as a team. Children generally find it more fun to play with at least one partner, for then they can take turns laying down rubber bands.

Each team gets a geoboard and draws a card from top of shuffled deck. Card tells team how many rubber bands to use.

Stage One: Children take turns placing rubber bands on geoboard. At this stage they just need to put all rubber bands on geoboard, and make sure each rubber band forms a straight line segment (see p.30 for example). You may need to help children lay down their rubber bands at first.

Stage Two: Children take rubber bands off board. Then they put the same number back on one at a time, taking turns. This time, tell them they are making a long snake. Have children refer to starting point of first rubber band laid down as tail of snake, and end point of last rubber band as head of snake. There are three restrictions in making this snake (see p.30 for example).

a) Once first rubber band is laid down, each successive rubber band begins on peg where last rubber band ended.

b) No rubber bands may overlap at any point other than endpoints.

c) No rubber bands may cross.

Stage Three: Leaving rubber bands on board, students manipulate rubber bands so tail of snake meets head (see p.30). Restrictions on this stage are:

a) The only rubber bands that may be moved are those containing the head and tail.

b) Only tail and head ends of these rubber bands may be moved, and they may be moved to any peg, as long as ...

c) No rubber band crosses any other rubber band.

Tell children that once they complete Stage Three, they have made a polygon. Polygon means a straight-sided, flat, closed figure.

Stage Four: Once children make first polygons, have them take all rubber bands off board and try to make another polygon with same number of rubber bands (see p.30).

Extensions:

1 Have children make smallest possible polygon with same number of rubber bands by making the bands less taut.

2 Have children make largest possible polygon with same number of rubber bands by stretching rubber bands.

3 Draw two cards instead of one. Child who draws larger number makes a big polygon with that many rubber bands; child who draws smaller number makes polygon with that many rubber bands inside larger polygon. Example: If cards drawn are 6 and 3, one child makes a hexagon, then other child tries to make a triangle inside a hexagon. This is a cooperative activity.

4 Draw a card. That many children lie down and make a polygon with each child playing the role of a rubber band. Other children may want to sketch outline of polygon created.

1 What happens to a rubber band the more you stretch it? **A: It becomes both longer and thinner.**

2 What do you have to do to the rubber bands to move from Stage 1 to Stage 2? From Stage 2 to Stage 3? From Stage 3 to Stage 4?
A: Answers will vary, but here are some things you're likely to hear: Stage 1 - 2: Join end of each rubber band to beginning of another rubber band. Stage 2 - 3: Snake has to eat its tail — or you make an inside and an outside. Stage 3 - 4: Start all over again and make a new shape with the same rubber bands — or make another snake eating its tail.

3 How can you tell if a figure is a polygon? **A: Snake must be eating its tail, and no part of snake may cross any other part of snake.**

4 How can you tell if a figure is not a polygon? **A: It's not a polygon if the snake is not eating its tail or if one part of snake crosses another part of snake.**

TIPS AND POINTERS

1 If children have not previously worked with geoboards, you may want to give them time for free play. Children often enjoy making letters, especially the first letters of their names.

2 As children work through the stages of the game, it helps to model the steps using a translucent geoboard that shows up on an overhead projector.

3 Children may initially find it easier to use cards from 3s through 6s. Once they get the idea, they can use all cards from 3s through 8s.

4 It's fun to use the geoboard paper to record the shapes each team creates.

ROUNDUP

FOR EACH CHILD OR GROUP OF CHILDREN:

➥ Deck of all numbered cards from 3 through 6 to start, then 3 through 8 for more advanced play.

➥ Geoboards and rubber bands. Use geoboards with 11 pegs on each side. It's best to have rubber bands of various sizes and colors. You can find these in the geoboard section of school supply stores or catalogs.

➥ Handout on p.30 to help children understand what each of the four stages looks like.

➥ OPTIONAL: "Polygon or Not?" and "Concave or Convex?" worksheets (pp.32-33) to deepen children's concepts of polygon, concave, and convex.

Tail-Eating Snakes: The Four Stages

Stage 1

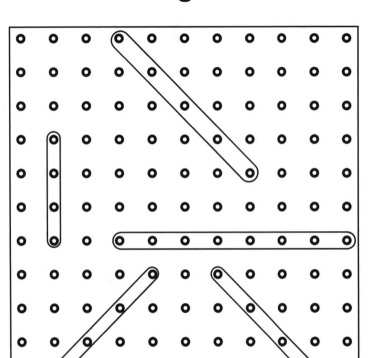

Stage 2

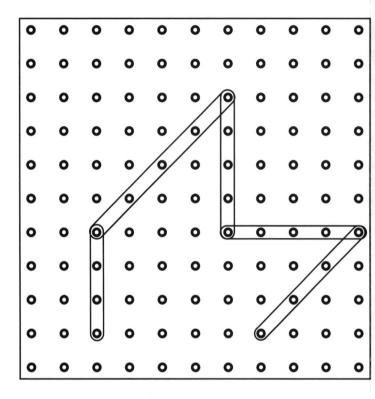

Stage 3

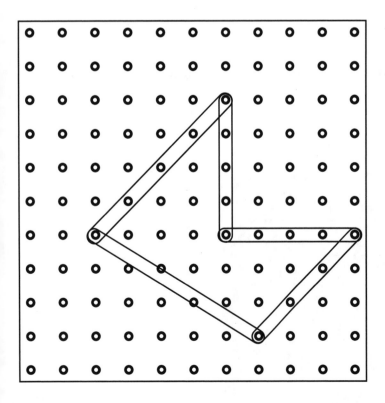

Stage 4

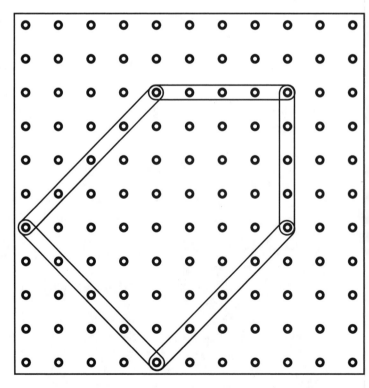

Tail-Eating Snakes: Notes for Educator

DIFFERENCE BETWEEN CONCAVE AND CONVEX POLYGONS:

A polygon is concave if you can find two points inside the polygon and draw a line segment connecting them that falls partly outside the polygon.

Drawings below show how this "two-point" test works.

Convex Polygons

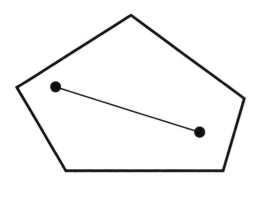

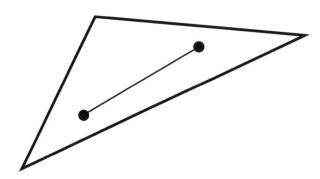

Segment between **ANY** two interior points stays entirely within the figure.

Concave Polygons

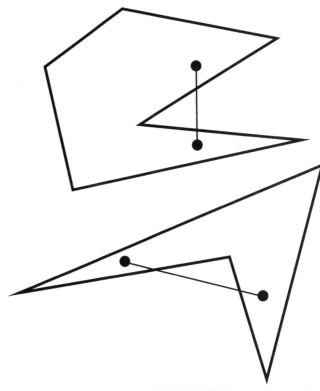

Segment between **CERTAIN** interior points falls partly outside the figure.

Suggestions for using worksheets on following two pages:
"Polygon ... Or not?"   and   "Concave or Convex?"

1st) As overhead or worksheet w/all children, to introduce concept.

2nd) As overhead or worksheet: children come up and try to prove whether a given figure is or isn't a polygon, or whether polygon is concave or convex using the two-point test.

3rd) As worksheet: use it to check for understanding. Individually, or in teams.

Answers to: Polygon ... Or not?

Only a, e and f are polygons.

b: one segment extends beyond vertex
c: not closed (snake not eating tail)
d: two segments extend beyond vertices
g: has a rounded side, but all sides of polygons must be
   straight line segments

Answers to: Concave or Convex?

a, e, and f are concave.
The other polygons are convex.

Children should use the "two-point" test
to confirm this.

Polygon? ... or Not?

Ring the figures that are polygons.
How do you know they are polygons?
How do you know that the other figures are not polygons?

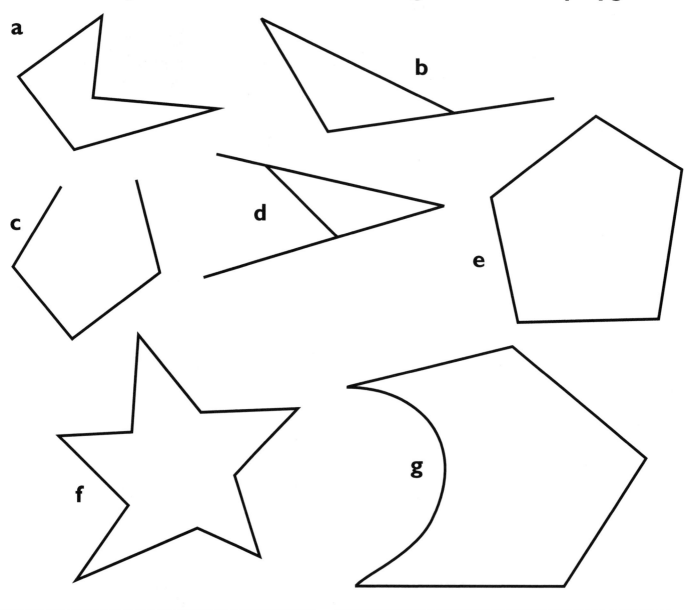

a

b

c

d

e

f

g

Draw your own polygon

Draw your own non-polygon

Concave or Convex?

Ring all the polygons that are concave.
Use the two-point test to check.

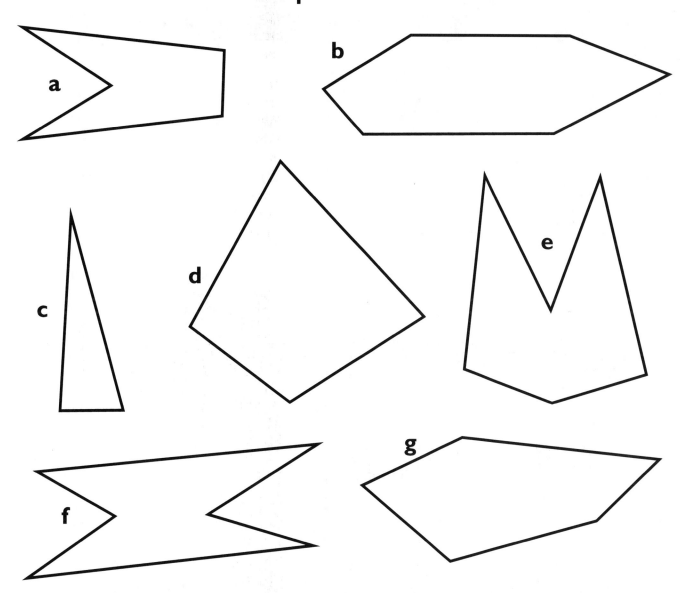

a

b

c

d

e

f

g

Draw your own concave polygon	Draw your own convex polygon

Relaxing beneath a big Western sky, young buckaroos gaze at clouds and compare the shapes they see in them. In this fun, open-ended game, children use their imagination to create artistic pictures, all the while learning about those straight-edged critters called polygons.

CONCEPT CORRAL

GEOMETRY:

➤ Identify polygons by the number of sides and corners they have.

➤ Create polygons using hands-on materials.

➤ Label polygons by name.

➤ Differentiate squares from diamonds (aka rhombuses).

CONNECTIONS

➤ Link concepts of various polygons to everyday objects.

REPRESENTATION

➤ Make models of various kinds of polygons.

Cloud Dreamin'

GAME A — Cooperative

GOAL: To create polygons and to associate their shapes with shapes of everyday objects.

 # Players: Any number.

1 Each child takes a turn selecting a card from deck, reading number on card, and collecting that many toothpicks. i.e. If child draws a 3 of diamonds, she collects three toothpicks; if she draws a 6 of spades, she collects six toothpicks. The number is all that matters, not the suit.

2 Children then look at the Cloud Dreamin' Flashcards sheet on p.37 to view examples of polygons formed with the number of sides indicated on their cards. i.e. If child draws a 5, she looks at the examples of pentagons since pentagons have five sides.

3 Each child uses her toothpicks to create a polygon with the number of sides on her card. Have children glue their toothpicks onto a piece of paper or oak tag.

4 Each child then uses art supplies (crayons, markers, etc.) to decorate polygon so it depicts an object from real life. i.e. Triangle may be an ice-cream cone or a tent; square may be a gift, window, etc.

5 Once children make their creations, have them attach a label from the Label Master on p.39 to display name of polygon.

6 It's fun for children to get up and tell everyone the formal name of their polygon (triangle, hexagon, etc.) and to show what shape they made it into.

GAME B — Cooperative

GOAL: For a child to arrange other children into the shape of a particular polygons.

 # Players: Between 5 and 7.

1 This game can be played with any number of children, and children take turns being the "architect".

2 Architect selects a card, and reads out the number on it. Architect then selects that many children to become the sides of the polygon.

3 The architect helps the children decide where to lie and position their bodies to create the polygon.

4 The rest of the class can help count sides and corners to make sure the polygon has been made correctly.

Note: for questions 5 through 9, children will need toothpicks to test their ideas.

1 Which kind of polygon could you relate to many objects? **A: Answers will vary.**

2 Which kind of polygon were you unable to relate to objects? **A: Answers will vary.**

3 Which polygon was easiest to make? Why? **A: Answers will vary.**

4 Which polygon was hardest to make? Why? **A: Answers will vary.**

5 Could you ever make a polygon with a different number of sides than corners? In other words, a polygon with four sides and five corners? Or with four corners and five sides? Or with three corners and 10 sides? Whatever answer you come up with, can you give a reason why you think this is true? **A: Every polygon must have the same number of sides and corners. It's impossible to make a polygon with different numbers of sides and corners. Try it and see.**

6 Do you remember the idea of concave polygons from Tail-Eating Snakes (pp. 28-33)? Recalling that concept and using just toothpicks all the same length, can you make a concave triangle? A concave quadrilateral? A concave pentagon? A concave hexagon? **A: It's impossible to make a concave triangle or quadrilateral. But children can make concave pentagons and hexagons. See pentagons and hexagons on Cloud Dreamin' Flashcards for examples.**

7 If all sides of the polygon have the same length, how many differently shaped triangles can you make with three toothpicks? **A: Only one, and it's a regular polygon — an equilateral triangle.**

8 If all four sides of a quadrilateral have the same length, how many differently shaped quadrilaterals can you make? How many differently shaped squares? **A: You can make only one square because all the angles are the same since they are all right angles. But there's no limit to how many differently shaped diamonds (rhombuses) you can make. A rhombus is a quadrilateral with all four sides the same length.**

9 If all five sides of a pentagon have the same length, how many differently shaped pentagons can you make? How about hexagons? **A: There's no limit to how many differently shaped pentagons or hexagons you can make. Try it and see for yourself.**

ROUNDUP

FOR EACH CHILD OR GROUP OF CHILDREN:

➠ One deck of all numbered cards from 3 through 6.

➠ Toothpicks, popsicle sticks (or some other straight object), and glue.

➠ Drawing paper or oak tag that children will glue their shapes onto.

➠ Crayons, markers, or colored pencils.

➠ One copy of the Cloud Dreamin' Flashcards on p.37 to give children examples of the shapes they can make.

➠ Cloud Dreamin' labels from the Label Master on p.39 to let children label their polygons.

➠ OPTIONAL: one copy of the Squares and Diamonds Worksheet on p.38 to reinforce the difference between these two kinds of quadrilaterals.

1 Since this game relies on a grasp of concept of polygon, it's a good follow-up to Tail-Eating Snakes.

2 To shorten and simplify game, use Cloud Dreamin' Flashcards sheet, copied off master on p.37. Children can simply draw a card and find shape with correct number of sides and corners. Then they can draw that shape.

3 Have children use glue or glue stick to attach their toothpicks to drawing paper or oak tag.

4 To reinforce names of polygons, run off labels on Cloud Dreamin' Label Master for children to label their polygons.

5 You may want each child to divide paper or oak tag into four sections so children know they will make four shapes in this activity.

6 The Squares and Diamonds Worksheet on p.38 gives children a chance to learn that they can make two kinds of quadrilaterals and to distinguish between these two kinds of figures.

Cloud Dreamin' Flashcards

Triangle

3 sides
3 corners

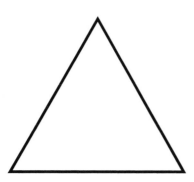
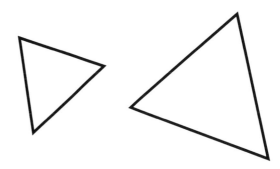

Quadri-lateral

4 sides
4 corners

Pentagon

5 sides
5 corners

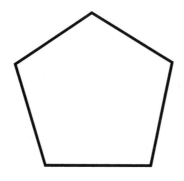
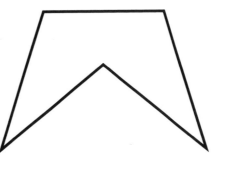
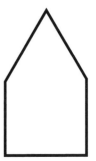

Hexagon

6 sides
6 corners

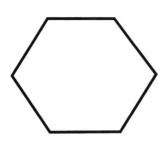
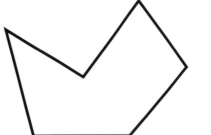

Cloud Dreamin'
Squares and Diamonds Worksheet

Square turning into a diamond

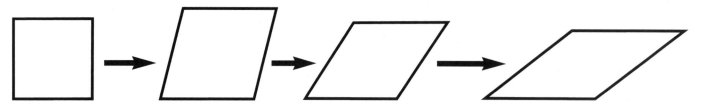

Diamond turning into a square

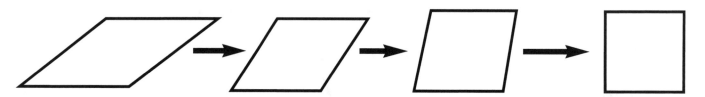

Which are diamonds? Which are squares?
Ring the squares to show the difference between the two shapes.

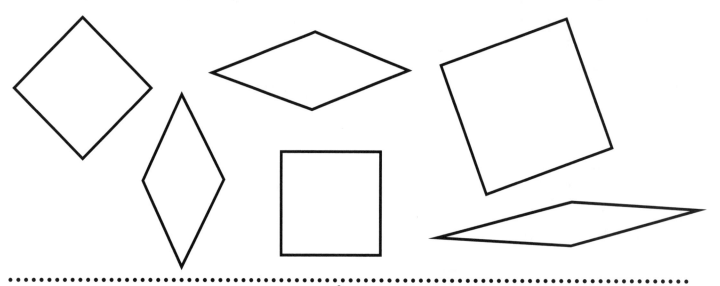

__Draw a diamond__ | __Draw a square__

Triangle

Quadrilateral

Pentagon

Hexagon

Galloping Guesses

GAME A Cooperative

GOAL: To make as many correct guesses as possible about whether a face-down card is red or black.

 # Players: 1, 2, 3, or 4.

1 Deck of 20 cards is shuffled and placed on table face down. One child begins by guessing if top card is black or red. After guessing, this child turns top card over where all can see it.

2 All children record whether that guess was right or wrong on Galloping Guesses Data Sheet. Players first locate the space corresponding to card turned over. Example: If card is 6 of diamonds, find space for 6 of ♦. If card is 6 of spades, find space for the 6 of ♠. If guess is right, players add a smile to face; if guess is wrong, children add a frown to face.

3 Play continues until all 20 cards have been guessed and turned over.

4 Once all 20 cards are turned over, players count number of correct guesses and write it on line at bottom of Data Sheet.

GAME B Competitive

GOAL: To make the most correct guesses about whether the cards are red or black.

 # Players: 2 or 4. With 4, you may want to play pair vs. pair.

Same rules as in Game A, only now each child or pair of children tries to make more correct guesses than her opponent(s).

1 How many correct guesses would you make if you guess all black or all red for all 20 cards? **A: You would get exactly 10 correct guesses.**

2 Can it help you to think about the information on your worksheet before you guess? How can this help you make a better guess? **A: Yes. By looking at the information, you can make a better guess. For example, if you can tell from your Data Sheet that there are five cards left, and that four of them must be black, then it makes more sense to guess black than red.**

3 Can you think of any situations in everyday life when you need to guess? Is there any information that can help you make the best guess possible? **A: Answers will vary.**

ROUNDUP

FOR EACH PLAYER OR GROUP OF PLAYERS:

➤ **All cards from ace through 10 in one black suit and all cards from ace through 10 in one red suit. Example: Use all 10 cards from ace of spades through 10 of spades and all 10 cards from ace of hearts through 10 of hearts.**

➤ **One copy of Galloping Guesses Data Sheet (copied off master on p.42) per child.**

TIPS AND POINTERS

1 For individual play, child guesses and records all by himself. If 2, 3, or 4 play cooperatively, each child takes a turn guessing and turning over a card while all children record on their own Galloping Guesses Data Sheet. If children play competitively, goal is to make more correct guesses than opposing team.

2 Before children play, it helps to model how to record guesses on the Data Sheet. Tell children that they first find the space on the Data Sheet corresponding to the turned-over card, and only then do they record — with an upturned mouth ("happy face") for a correct guess, or a downturned mouth ("sad face") for an incorrect guess.

3 It also helps to "think aloud" as you demonstrate the game to bring out its process-of-elimination aspects. Some useful questions to ask aloud include:

➤ How many black cards have been played?

➤ Knowing that there are 10 black cards altogether, can we figure out how many blacks are left?

➤ Of the cards that are left, can we figure out how many are black and how many are red?

➤ Can this information help us make a good guess?

4 Educators may remind children to stop and count the number of cards of each color before making guesses.

Galloping Guesses Data Sheet

RED CARDS				BLACK CARDS			
A	♥	or	♦	A	♣	or	♠
2	♥	or	♦	2	♣	or	♠
3	♥	or	♦	3	♣	or	♠
4	♥	or	♦	4	♣	or	♠
5	♥	or	♦	5	♣	or	♠
6	♥	or	♦	6	♣	or	♠
7	♥	or	♦	7	♣	or	♠
8	♥	or	♦	8	♣	or	♠
9	♥	or	♦	9	♣	or	♠
10	♥	or	♦	10	♣	or	♠

Number of correct guesses: _____

STORYLINE

Before the campfire is lit, young cowpokes go hunting for two or more numbers that combine to make a third number. Whoever collects the most cards gets the best grub. Yummy! Beans, ribs, and all the fixins!

CONCEPT CORRAL

NUMBER & OPERATION

➤ Find two numbers that add to a third number.

➤ Find three or more numbers that add to another number.

➤ Find the numbers that form a subtraction sentence.

REASONING

➤ Figure out how to take the most cards on any given turn.

CONNECTIONS

➤ Discover links between addition and subtraction.

Pre-req skill: Children need familiarity with both number concept and basic addition.

Hunting for Grub

GAME A Cooperative

GOAL: To get the best grub by finding two numbers that add to a third number.

 # Players: 1, 2, 3, or 4 (can be played in a solitary fashion — a fun activity for children who finish assignments early).

1 Shuffle cards and place deck face down. Take four cards off top of deck and place them face up in middle of table.

2 Children look at the upturned cards, searching for any two that add up to any other. Example: If upturned cards are: **7 1 3 & 4**, children can combine the **3** and **4** to make **7**, and say: **3 + 4 = 7**. Children would place these three cards to the side. (See Sample Game master on p.47.) Children can also write this fact down on Addition Worksheet A.

3 If children cannot make a number sentence, each child takes a turn turning over one card at a time until children find and make a number sentence.

4 Every time children make a number sentence, they put three additional cards face up and try to make another number sentence. This is true even if putting out three cards makes the number of face-up cards more than four. As a result, the number of face-up cards will at all times be four or more.

5 Play continues until children run through all cards in deck. At end, children count cards to see how many they collected. In this way, they compete against themselves by trying to collect more and more cards each time they run through the deck.

Option: After going through deck, children may enjoy setting goals corresponding to various meal tickets. i.e. Collecting 20 cards = Campfire Feast; collecting 15 cards = Scout Meal, etc.

GAME B Competitive

GOAL: To get the best grub by finding two numbers that add to a third number, but in competition with other buckaroos.

 # Players: 2, 3, or 4. With 4, play everyone for herself, or pair vs. pair.

1 First player looks at the four upturned cards and tries to make a number sentence.

2a If player cannot do so, she turns next card in deck face up, and it becomes opponent's turn to try to make a sentence.

2b If player does make a sentence, she states her fact. i.e. **3+ 4 = 7**.

3 After a player makes a number sentence, she turns over the next three cards from the top of deck and places them face up to replace cards she took. Then opponent takes a turn.

4 Play continues in this fashion until all cards in deck are used.

5 After all cards are played, children count their cards. They award themselves meal tickets based on who got the most cards (Campfire Feast), second most (Scout Meal), third most (Young Rustler Leftovers), and least (Barrel-Bottom Stew).

GAME C
Cooperative

GOAL: To get the best grub by finding two or more numbers that add to a third number.

 # Players: 1, 2, 3, or 4.

Same basic rules as Game A but with these differences:

1 Now children place six cards face up.

2 Now children may use more than two addends to make a set. Example: If cards showing are: **1   2   4   5   8   &   10**, a child could add the **1, 2** and **5** to make **8**. In such a case, player would take all four of those cards. (See Sample Game master on p.47.) Reason for using six cards is to increase chances that children find more than two addends.

3 Whichever player makes a sentence turns over as many cards from the deck as she took — to create new options for next player.

GAME D
Competitive

GOAL: To get the best grub by finding two or more numbers that add to a third number, but in competition with other buckaroos.

 # Players: 2, 3, or 4. With four, play either everyone for herself, or pair vs. pair.

Same competitive goal and rules as in Game B, except that now players may put out six cards to start, and they may use two or more addends to make a set, as in Game C. Meal cards awarded as in Game B.

CAMPFIRE CHAT

1 What kind of upturned cards make it easier to create number sentences? Why? **A: A mixture of higher and lower cards with more lower than higher. Lower cards serve as addends; higher cards can be the sum.**

2 What kind of upturned cards makes it harder to create number sentences? Why? **A: In general, high cards make it hard to make a**

ROUNDUP

FOR EACH CHILD OR GROUP OF CHILDREN:

➤ One deck of cards with all picture cards removed. Ace stands for the number 1. If you wish, let Joker stand for 0. Using the Joker here allows children to make number sentences like 7 + 0 = 7, and 9 - 0 = 9.

➤ Sample Game master on p.47 helps children understand the rules of play.

➤ Hunting for Grub Meal Tickets copied off master on p.48 add a fun element.

➤ For Games A and B, you may want children to use manipulative counters and/or Addition Worksheet A on p.94.

➤ For Games C and D, you may want children to use manipulative counters and/or Addition Worksheet B on p.95.

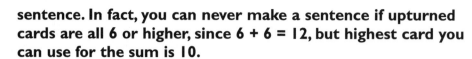

sentence. In fact, you can never make a sentence if upturned cards are all 6 or higher, since 6 + 6 = 12, but highest card you can use for the sum is 10.

3 Is there any pattern to the number of cards you can collect in Games A and B? If so, why would this pattern exist? **A: Number of cards collected is always a multiples of three, for in Games A and B there are always three cards in each number sentence.**

4 Do your subtraction number sentences look anything like your addition number sentences? **A: The three numbers often appear in a reverse left-to-right fashion. i.e. 3 + 4 = 7 vs. 7 - 4 = 3.**

5 In Games C or D, did you ever first think of one way to make a set, then think of another way that would bring you more cards? **A: Answers will vary.**

6 Does this game show you anything about addition that you hadn't realized before? If so, what new things have you learned? **A: Answers will vary.**

TIPS AND POINTERS

1 Model how to put together number sentences before letting children play. Stress that both the addends and the sum are found among the face-up cards. Example: If in Game A the four upturned cards are: **1 7 3 & 4**, show children that they can add the **3** and the **4** to make **7**, creating the sentence: **3 + 4 = 7**.

2 It's easiest if you first play this game as a pure addition game. As a later challenge, encourage children to name their subtraction facts as well. i.e. If face-up cards in Game A are: **7 1 3 & 4**, children first state the addition fact: **3 + 4 = 7.** With time and practice, they can also state a corresponding subtraction fact like **7 - 4 = 3.** Similarly, if cards in Game C are: **1 3 4 5 9 10**, children can first state an addition fact: **5 + 3 + 1 = 9.** With practice, they can eventually state a corresponding subtraction fact, like: **9 - 1 - 3 = 5**

3 You may want children to record their number sentences on the addition or subtraction worksheets mentioned in the Roundup.

4 You may also want children to check their number sentences either by making a quick drawing or by using counting manipulatives.

Extension: If in time children find game easy, add a fun twist by allowing them to make two different number sentences at one time, if there are enough cards. Example: If upturned cards are: **2 4 5 6 8** and **9**, children could make two number sentences: **2 + 6 = 8** and **4 + 5 = 9**, and thereby take six cards in one turn.

Hunting for Grub
Sample Game Master

Game A or Game B

Cards showing:

You can take:

Because ... **+** **=** **(5 + 2 = 7)**

- -

Game C or Game D

Cards showing:

You can take:

Because ... **+** **+** **=** **(4 + 4 + 1 = 9)**

Hunting for Grub
Meal Ticket Master

Campfire Feast

All you can eat of beans, bar-b-que ribs, honey-glazed prairie chicken, cornbread with orange marmalade, apple pie with ice cream, and hot chocolate too.

Scout Meal

A hefty plate of beans, a side of ribs, cornbread and cowboy coffee (ground coffee beans in hot water).

Young Rustler Leftovers

Boiled pig's feet, a hunk of cornbread, a cold baked potato, and a tin cup full of hot water.

Barrel-Bottom Stew

A "tasty" mixture of hot water with rib and pig drippings.

Stuck in the Mud

GAME A Competitive

GOAL: To get to safety by grabbing the Tree Branch at space 14 — or to be the one player who has not fallen into the the Mudpit after all others have fallen in.

 # Players: 2, 3, or 4. With 4, it's fun to play pair vs. pair.

1 Shuffle deck, place it face down and lay it where everyone may take cards off the top. Each player puts a token on space **7** on any of the four pathways on the Stuck in the Mud Gameboard.

2 First player takes top card and turns it over. Card's number tells how many spaces to move, and its suit color tells which direction to move in. If suit is red, player moves token that many spaces down — toward Mudpit. If suit is black, player moves token that many spaces up — away from Mudpit.

3 If player reaches the 14 space, she is rescued by the overhanging Tree Branch and stops playing. But play continues for the other players.

4 Two ways to win, and more than one player may win:
a) if a child gets to safety by reaching the Tree Branch at space 14, or
b) if all the other players have fallen into the Mudpit and a child is the last player left.

5 When you run out of cards, shuffle deck to ensure you don't repeat the last run of cards.

CAMPFIRE CHAT

1 How can you tell if you might win or lose on the next card? In other words, how can you tell if you're in the "Danger Zone"?
A: You're in the "Danger Zone" if you are on space 1, 2, 3, or 4. That's because any red card could plunge you into the Mudpit.

2 How can you tell if you might win on the next card? In other words, how can you tell if you're in the "Safety Zone"? **A: You're in the "Safety Zone" if you are on space 10, 11, 12, or 13. That's because any black card could allow you to reach safety at the Tree Branch.**

3 Is there a number that corresponds to the Mudpit? If so, what number would it be? **A: Yes, the number 0 corresponds to the Mudpit.**

TIPS AND POINTERS

1 You'll want to demonstrate how to move tokens before letting children play. Stress that children count the number of MOVES they make, but NOT the space they start on (a common mistake for young counters). So if they are on **7** and draw a black **2**, they count one for MOVING from **7** to **8**, and they count one for MOVING from **8** to **9**. The fact is: **7 + 2 = 9**. Many children mistakenly think they first count the **7**, then move to the **8**, and they come out with the incorrect fact: **7 + 2 = 8**. Stressing that children count moves helps eliminate this misconception.

2 Since this game lays a foundation for the number line concept, you may want to follow up with a number line lesson. If you've already introduced the number line, this game provides a fun, follow-up/reinforcement activity.

3 You may want children to state math facts either before or after they move their tokens. This helps keep emphasis of the game on math facts, not just on moving. For example, if a player is at **10** and draws a black **3**, she says: **10 + 3 = 13**. If the player is at **10** and draws a red **4**, he says: **10 - 4 = 6**. Players can either move, then say the fact; or say the fact, then move.

4 You might want to write this somewhere everyone can see it: **BLACK means + / RED means —**. Or for children unfamiliar with subtraction: **BLACK means UP / RED means DOWN**.

5 You may also want children to write their facts as they play.

6 This game can be used to provide an introduction to positive and negative numbers. You may want to bring this out by saying that black cards are "positive" and red cards are "negative".

7 If you have enough cards, double deck size by using cards from two decks. This allows children to play more and shuffle less.

ROUNDUP

FOR EACH GROUP OF CHILDREN:

➤ **One deck of cards with all the aces, 2s, 3s, and 4s.**

➤ **One "Stuck in the Mud" Gameboard copied off the master on p.52.**

➤ **One small token per player for moving on the board (small buttons work well).**

Stuck in the Mud!!! Gameboard

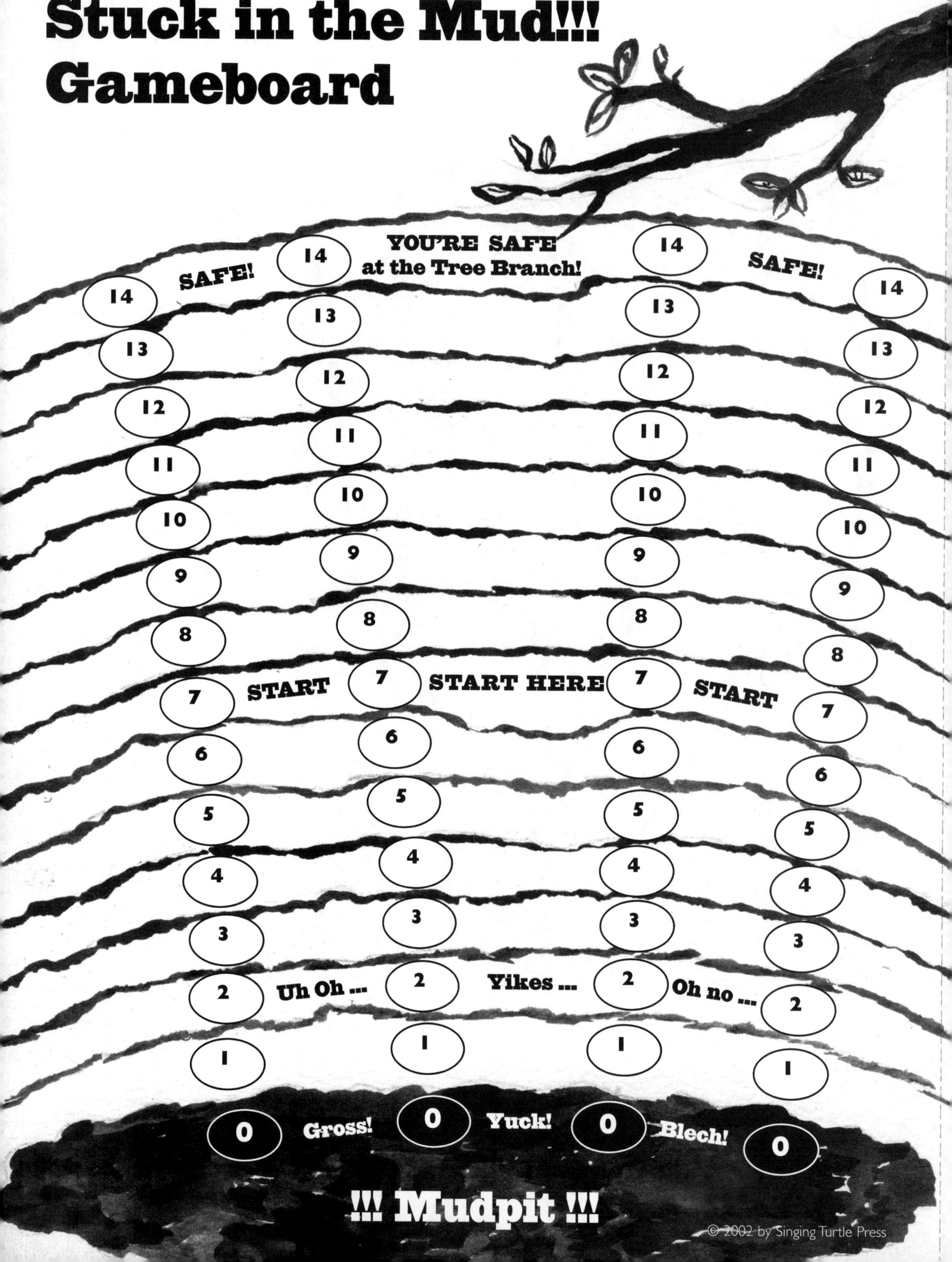

SAFE!

14

YOU'RE SAFE at the Tree Branch!

14

SAFE!

14

13

13

13

13

12

12

12

12

11

11

11

11

10

10

10

10

9

9

9

9

8

8

8

8

7 **START** 7 **START HERE** 7 **START** 7

6 6 6 6

5 5 5 5

4 4 4 4

3 3 3 3

2 **Uh Oh ...** 2 **Yikes ...** 2 **Oh no ...** 2

1 1 1 1

0 **Gross!** 0 **Yuck!** 0 **Blech!** 0

!!! Mudpit !!!

Mysterious Bandit

Mysterious Bandits are on the loose, robbing money from banks, trains, and innocent frontier people. Young buckaroos get deputized and try to capture these dastardly bandits. To do so, they need to figure out the missing number in addition sentences. Each number they figure out means that another member of the Mysterious Bandit posse is locked away.

CONCEPT CORRAL

NUMBER & OPERATION
➡ Add whole numbers.

ALGEBRA
➡ Figure out the value of a variable.

PROBLEM SOLVING
➡ Develop strategies for discovering the value of a variable.

REASONING
➡ Explain how to discover the value of a variable.

CONNECTIONS
➡ Discover links between addition and subtraction.

GAME A Cooperative

GOAL: To nab Mysterious Bandits by discovering their identity.

 # Players: 1, 2, 3, or 4. Students can play this game individually or in cooperative groups.

1 Educator sets a goal for how many Bandit Badges children must collect to win. Educator also makes either a copy or a transparency of Mysterious Bandit Worksheet A, B, or C, depending on level students are ready for.

2 Using the worksheet, educator sets up an addition sentence for all students to see. This can be done on an overhead projector by making a transparency of the worksheet and laying transparent playing cards (see final item on Roundup) on top of it. Or educator may make the number sentence on the paper worksheet, putting it on a desk and letting children gather round.

3 Children look at problem and try to figure out the identity of the face-down card, the "Mysterious Bandit," individually, in pairs, or in cooperative groups.

4 Every time children correctly figure out the value of the face-down card, educator awards them with one Bandit Badge from the master on p.57.

5 Encourage children to explain their reasoning after giving answers. Educator may wish to bring out children's reasoning through questions and discussion.

6 Children win when they collect as many Mysterious Bandit Badges as educator establishes as goal.

GAME B Competitive

GOAL: To be the sheriff who saves the day and nabs all Mysterious Bandits before opponent sheriff beats you to the punch.

 # Players: 2 or 4. With 4, it's best to play pair vs. pair. You may want children to alternate partners round-robin style.

1 Educator sets goal of how many Bandit Badges children must collect to win. Educator also makes copies of Mysterious Bandit Worksheet A, B, or C on pp.58-60 depending on level students are ready for — and gives one worksheet to each pair or group playing.

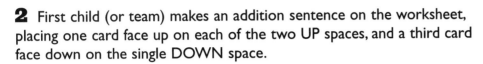

2 First child (or team) makes an addition sentence on the worksheet, placing one card face up on each of the two UP spaces, and a third card face down on the single DOWN space.

3 By studying number sentence, other child (or team) tries to figure out the value of the Mysterious Bandit card. This child declares what she believes to be the value of the Mysterious Bandit.

4 Child (or team) that created number sentence turns over the card.

5 If guessing child was correct, that child (or team) gets one Bandit Badge.

6 After the guess — whether right or wrong — children (or teams) switch roles, so that child who guessed now creates a number sentence, and vice-versa.

7 Play until one child or team wins by collecting the specified goal number of Bandit Badges.

CAMPFIRE CHAT

1 What strategy do you use to figure out the Mysterious Bandit on Worksheet A? On Worksheet B? On Worksheet C? **A: Some students will discover that they can use subtraction for Worksheets B and C. Others will describe the strategy of "counting up". i.e. In a problem like 2 + ___ = 7, they count up 5 from 2 to reach 7, and thereby know that the missing number is 5.**

2 Which worksheet makes it easiest to figure out the Mysterious Bandit? Why? Which one made it hardest? Why? **A: Children often say Worksheet A is easiest because all they have to do is add.**

3 Is anyone using subtraction to figure out the value of the Mysterious Bandit? If so, on which worksheet or worksheets do you use subtraction? Is there any similarity between addition and subtraction? If so, what similarity do you see? **A: Some children will note that on Worksheet B or C, they can subtract the face-up addend from the total to find the other addend. i.e. In a problem like 2 + ___ = 7, they can subtract 2 from 7 to get 5, the missing number.**

4 On Worksheet A, is it possible to use different face-up cards to get the same face-down card? Example: If face-down card is 8, is there only one pair of cards that equal 8, or are there many pairs of cards that equal 8? **A: Yes, it's possible to use different face-up cards to equal the same face-down card. i.e. If face-down card (the sum) is 8, you can use a variety of face-up cards, such as: 0 + 8; 1 + 7; 2 + 6; 3 + 5; 4 + 4; 5 + 3; 6 + 2; 7 + 1; and 8 + 0 — just as one example!**

ROUNDUP

FOR EACH CHILD OR GROUP:

➤ Deck with all picture cards removed. If you wish, use Joker to stand for 0. That allows children to learn the effect of 0 in addition sentences.

➤ Mysterious Bandit Addition Worksheets A, B, and C on pp.58-60. Teachers need to make either transparencies or copies, depending on whether children play Game A or Game B.

➤ Bandit Badges Master on p.57. Copy it, making enough badges so each group will have as many as they need. (See Tips & Pointer 3.)

➤ OPTIONAL: Transparent playing cards for overhead projector use. These may be purchased in educational supply catalogs, and they provide a great way to demonstrate this game — and other card games — to a large group.

5 On worksheets B and C, is it possible to use different face-up cards for the same face-down cards? Does this help you see any patterns in addition? **A: Yes, it is possible. Example: On Worksheet B, if face-down card is 3, you could create number sentences like: 1 + 3 = 4; 2 + 3 = 5; 3 + 3 = 6; 4 + 3 = 7; etc. One pattern in these number sentences is that the sum face-up card is always 3 more than the addend face-up card. i.e. 6 is 3 more than 3; 7 is 3 more than 4; etc. And it's no coincidence, for the problem involves adding 3 to the first addend to get the sum.**

TIPS AND POINTERS

1 Children usually find Worksheet A to be easiest, Worksheet B intermediate, and Worksheet C most difficult. It's generally best to use worksheets in order, starting with Worksheet A.

2 Game A is meant to introduce children to overall game concept. If students need extra practice before moving to Game B, here are three helpful approaches:

a) Start with easy problems by limiting cards used. Example: You may want to limit numbers you're adding to those from 1 through 3.

b) Use manipulative counters (buttons, pebbles, etc.) to help children count. Show a problem, then have children set it up with counters. Help children make transition from numbers shown on cards to number of counters. In some cases, children may want to touch-count the suit ikon. i.e. On 5 of diamonds, they may want to touch-count each of the five diamonds.

c) One way to demonstrate game concept is to use a combination of see-through and opaque cups with counters inside. Example: For the equation: 3 + DOWN = 7, set up two mats. Left mat has a see-through cup with 3 counters and an opaque cup with 4 counters. Right mat has a see-through cup with 7 counters. Tell children that both mats have same number of counters. Looking at cups, they try to figure out number of counters in opaque cup.

3 Educator establishes goal for how many Bandit Badges children must collect to win. Base this on children's skill and familiarity with game, but remain flexible. Number of Bandit Badges children need may vary from three to ten.

4 Suggest that children put their Bandit Badges in a central pile for all at their center. Then, as they win them in Game A, they can make a pile of the badges they have won. In Game B, each child makes a pile of the Bandit Badges she wins.

Bandit Badges Master

Found and Arrested

Marvin the Moustache

Found and Arrested

"Rowdy" Ramona

Found and Arrested

"Sweet-Tooth" Swen

Found and Arrested

"Hold-Up" Harriet

Found and Arrested

"Cheatin'" Charlie

Found and Arrested

"Pick-Pocket" Patty

Found and Arrested

Marvin the Moustache

Found and Arrested

"Rowdy" Ramona

Found and Arrested

"Sweet-Tooth" Swen

Found and Arrested

"Hold-Up" Harriet

Found and Arrested

"Cheatin'" Charlie

Found and Arrested

"Pick-Pocket" Patty

Mysterious Bandit Worksheet A

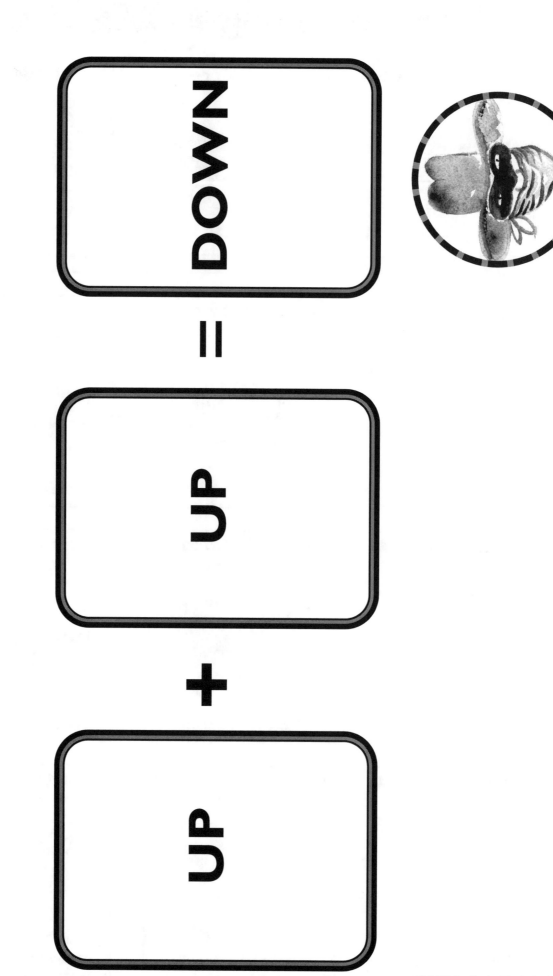

UP + UP = DOWN

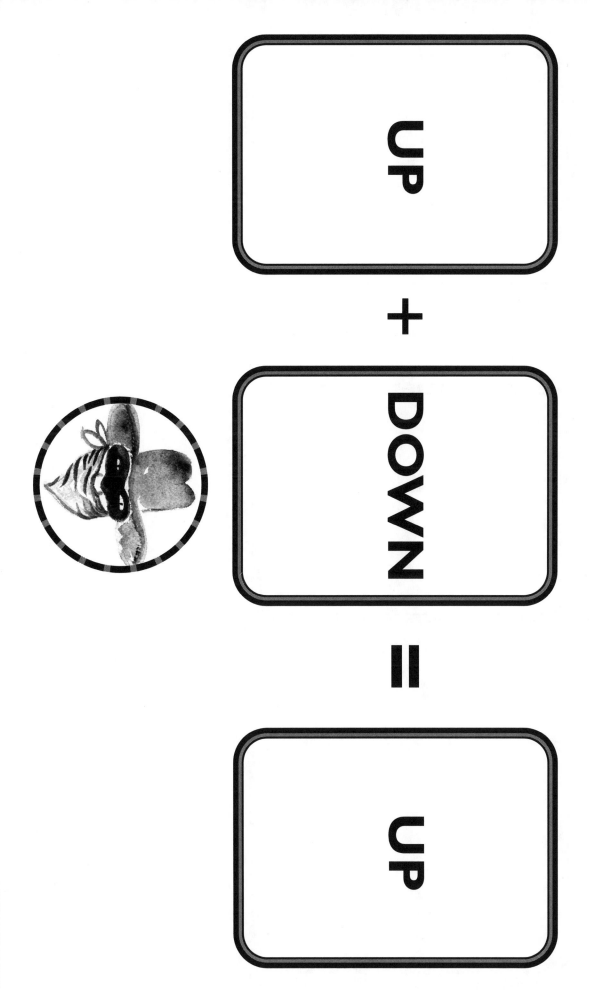

UP + DOWN = UP

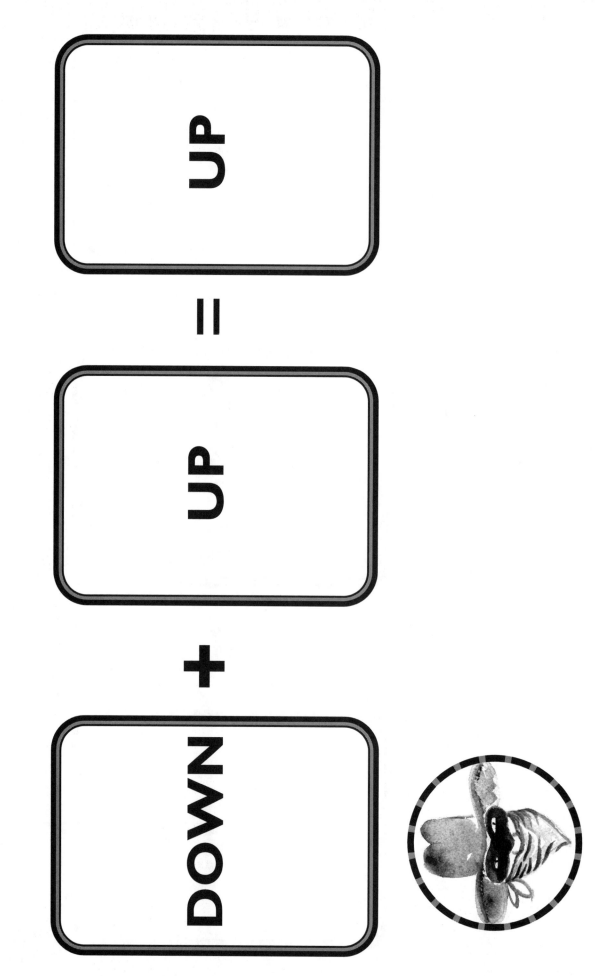

DOWN + UP = UP

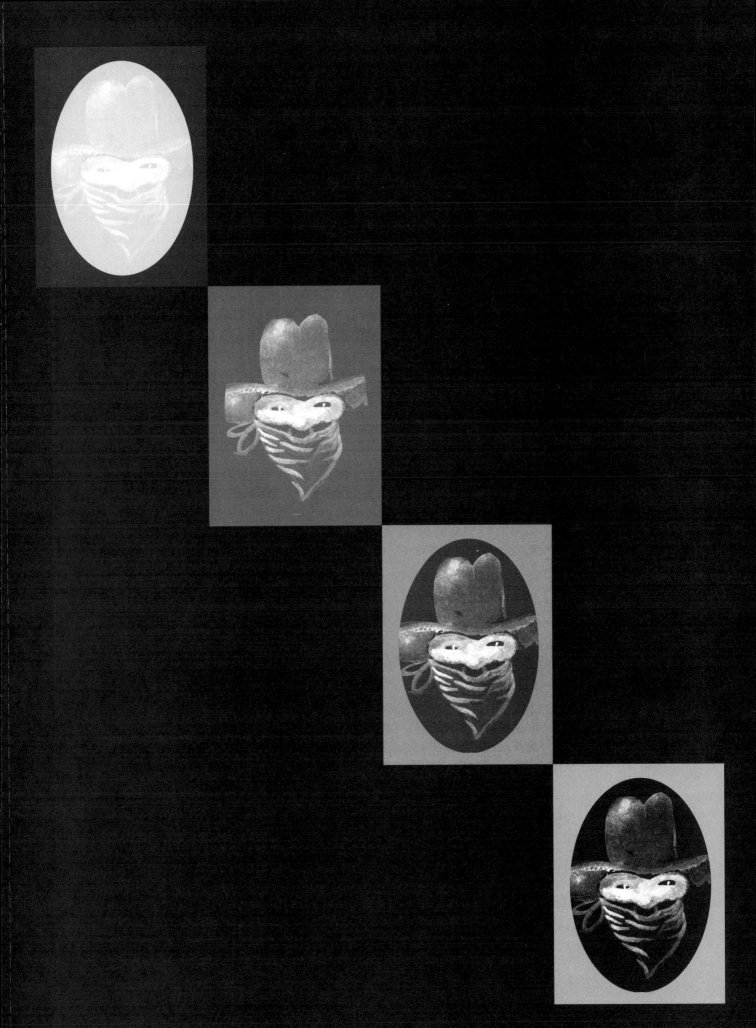

"Howdy Pardner!"

GAME A Cooperative

GOAL: To find a trail partner for the upcoming cattle drive by getting a sum that matches the sum of another player.

 # Players: 3, 4, or 5.

1 Dealer shuffles deck, places it face down on table, and gives each child one card face up. Each child writes number of this card in every **circle** on the left side of "Howdy Pardner!" Worksheet (the circular "Addend 1" space).

2 Dealer gives each child a second card face up and to the right of the first card, so that both cards are showing (see "Howdy Pardner!" Card Setup Sheet).

3 Children write number of second card in the **square** "Addend 2" box on worksheet. Children add value of their two cards and write answer in the **rectangular** "SUM" box. Children check if any of them have matching sums.

4a If no children have matching sums, Dealer gives each child another "Addend 2" card, placing it on top of previous "Addend 2" card. On next line of worksheet, children add new "Addend 2" card to "Addend 1" card. Again children check if any of them have matching sums.

4b When two or more children get matching sums, they become trail partners. They say "Howdy Pardner!" and shake hands.

5 As soon as two or more children become trail partners, the first round ends, the partnerships are dissolved, and all children get a fresh chance to find partners. To set up for next round, all children keep their single "Addend 1" card, but return their "Addend 2" pile to Dealer.

6 Dealer shuffles those cards, then gives each child a new "Addend 2" card to start next round.

7 Play continues until children fill in every number sentence on worksheet. TIP: Tell children that not all of them will get trail partners every time they go through the worksheet, for game involves a lot of chance.

8 This game is both an end in itself and a starting point for exploration of addition patterns. To help children explore addition patterns, explore Campfire Chat questions 1 - 6 after a worksheet gets filled up.

1 Once children fill out both sides of the "Howdy Pardner!" Worksheet, encourage them to look for patterns on their own individual worksheets. **A: Answers will vary, but children often notice that the second card and the sum are apart by the value of the first card. Example: If first card is a 2, then by viewing number sentences like: 2 + 3 = 5; 2 + 4 = 6; 2 + 5 = 7, children notice that the sum is always 2 more than the second card. i.e. The sum 5 is 2 more than 3; the sum 6 is 2 more than 4; etc. To help children see this pattern, have them arrange their number sentences with Addend 2 in ascending order, like this: 4 + 0 = 4; 4 + 1 = 5; 4 + 2 = 6; 4 + 3 = 7; 4 + 4 = 8; 4 + 5 = 9. You may want to do this on a chalkboard or an overhead for one child's number sentences to demonstrate the pattern.**

2 Is there any way that spotting this pattern can help you learn your addition facts? **A: Yes. Once you know the pattern, you know that if the number you're adding on is one more than the previous number you added, the new sum is one more than previous sum. Example: Suppose you just found out that 2 + 4 = 6. Given a new problem: 2 + 5, you would know that 2 + 5 is one more than 6, so 2 + 5 = 7.**

3 Once children see this pattern, they enjoy creating number sentences in ascending order even without the use of cards. Educator selects the first number, and then children create number sentences adding one more each time to that first number. **Example: Educator selects the number 3. Children write: 3 + 0 = 3; 3 + 1 = 4; 3 + 2 = 5; etc. They can also do this in descending order: 3 + 7 = 10; 3 + 6 = 9; 3 + 5 = 8; etc.**

4 Did it ever happen that two of you got the same sum with exactly opposite cards. Example: One child got 2 + 3, and another got 3 + 2, and they matched with 5 as their sum? **A: Answers will vary, but usually some children will recognize that this did happen in their game.**

5 If two numbers in an addition sentence are the same but in reverse order, will the sums of those sentences always be the same? Example: Does 4 + 2 = 2 + 4? does 3 + 5 = 3 + 5? **A: Yes, the order of the addends does not matter, for the sums will be the same. This is called the commutative property of addition.**

6 Now you see that the order of the numbers you're adding doesn't change the sum. How can this help you learn addition facts? **A: Yes, once you understand this aspect of addition, you know two facts for every one. Example: If you know that 2 + 7 = 9, you now also know that 7 + 2 = 9.**

7 When is your group more likely to get a set of trail partners earlier — if your group has more players, or if you have fewer players? And why? **A: Your group is more likely to get a trail partner earlier if it has more players. That's**

ROUNDUP

FOR EACH GROUP OF CHILDREN:

➠ **One deck with all cards from aces though 5s. Ace stands for the number 1; optional: add Joker, which stands for 0.**

➠ **One "Howdy Pardner!" Worksheet, copied off the master on p.66, for each child.**

➠ **OPTIONAL: "Howdy Pardner!" Card Setup Sheet, copied off the master on p.65, to help children arrange their cards.**

➠ **OPTIONAL: Manipulative counters to help children add numbers.**

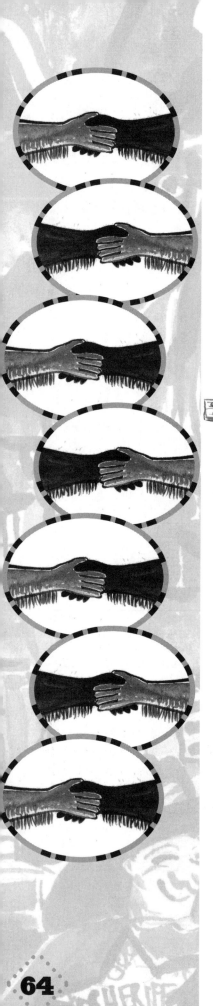

because the more players you have, the more chances there are that two or more of those players will get sums that match.

8 When is your group less likely to get a set of trail partners earlier — if you have more players, or if you have fewer players? And why? **A: Your group is less likely to get a trail partner earlier if it has fewer players. That's because the fewer players you have, the fewer chances there are that two or more of those players will get sums that match.**

9 If the cards you are playing with are the aces through 5s, what's the least number of players you need to be sure to get a match on every round? And why? **A: 10 players. Playing with the cards from aces through 5s, there are 9 possible sums: 2 (ace + ace) through 10 (5 + 5). The nine possible sums are therefore: 2, 3, 4, 5, 6, 7, 8, 9, and 10. So if you have 9 players, it's possible (though extremely unlikely) that each player gets a different sum. But as soon as you throw in a 10th player, that player must get a sum that is the same as one of the other player's sums. Try it and see!**

TIPS AND POINTERS

1 To conserve paper and make game last longer, copy "Howdy Pardner!" Worksheet onto both sides of each sheet of paper.

2 It helps to model game either on a desktop or using overhead projector.

3 When modeling game, show how to fill in "Howdy Pardner!" Worksheet. Make sure children know that when they get their first card, they should write its number in every circle on left side of page on both sides of worksheet. That way, all they have to do on each turn is fill in next two boxes.

4 Also model how to set up cards using the "Howdy Pardner!" Card Setup Sheet. Once children have experience using the sheet, they can abandon it. But the setup sheet helps them keep their two kinds of cards distinct.

5 Feel free to modify deck depending on children's ability. You may want to reduce deck to say, aces through 3s, or aces through 4s, for children new to adding. For children with more experience, include more cards than just aces through 5s.

6 Consider combining cards from two or more decks so children play more and shuffle less.

7 If children are new to adding, let them use manipulative counters to find sums.

8 Encourage children to say "Howdy Pardner!" and shake hands when they get matching sums or differences, for it makes the game more fun.

"Howdy Pardner!" Card Setup Sheet

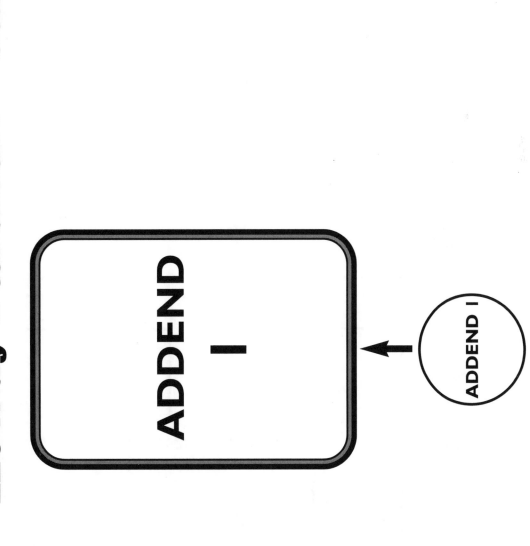

ADDEND 1

← ADDEND 1

KEEP THIS CARD HERE when filling out your worksheet.

Addend 2

← Addend 2

PUT EACH NEW CARD HERE.

"Howdy Pardner!" Worksheet

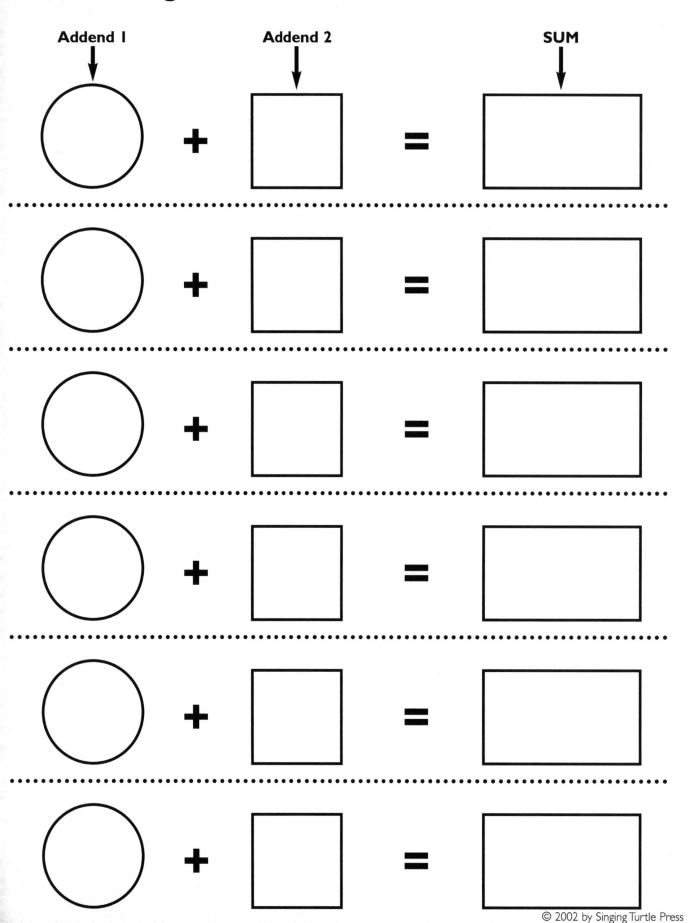

Addend 1   Addend 2   SUM

© 2002 by Singing Turtle Press

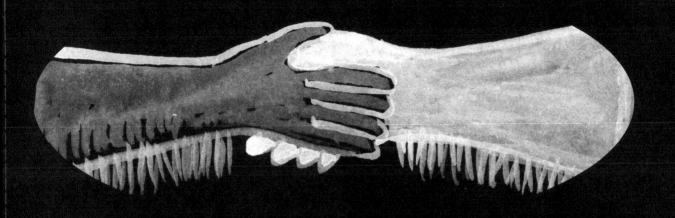

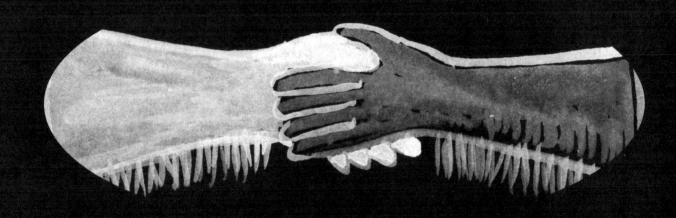

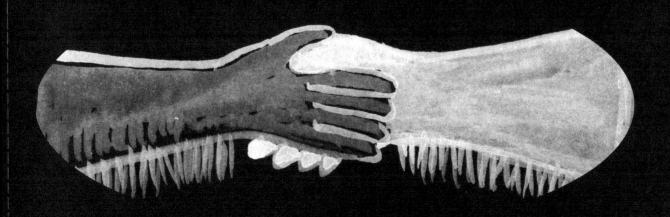

Just as a rancher sits down to supper, a steer breaks out of its pen. The rancher has to chase it up and down the ranchland, and the steer tries to get away through a "Broken Fence". Will the rancher capture the steer, or will the steer make it to freedom?

CONCEPT CORRAL

NUMBER & OPERATION
➡ Add and subtract along a number line.

ALGEBRA
➡ Develop foundation for concept of positive and negative numbers by moving tokens through northern spaces (positive numbers), across the zero space, and into southern spaces (negative numbers).

PROBLEM SOLVING
➡ Develop and test strategies for winning.

CONNECTIONS
➡ See ties between moving along a number line and using operations of addition and subtraction.

Steer on the Loose!

GAME A Competitive

GOAL: For the Rancher, to catch the Steer. For the Steer, to reach freedom through the "Broken Fence".

 # Players: 2 or 4. With 4, play pair vs. pair.

1 Both decks are shuffled and placed face down on Steer on the Loose! Card Layout Sheet: black cards on the "Black Pile" space, red cards on the "Red Pile" space. One child chooses to be Steer, other child chooses to be Rancher. If four play, one pair can be the Steer and make decisions together, and in same way other pair can be Rancher.

2 Rancher and Steer both place one token on the **0** position in their respective lanes.

3 Whichever player is the Steer chooses a card from either black or red pile. If player chooses a **black** card, she moves her token as many spaces **north** as indicated by number on card. i.e. **Black 3** tells her to move token **3 spaces up** — to the **3 north** space. If she chooses a **red** card, she moves token as many spaces **south** as indicated by number on card. i.e. **Red 2** tells her to move token **2 spaces down** — to the **2 south** space.

4 After Steer moves, Rancher picks one card from either pile with goal of landing on same position that Steer is now on.

5 Rancher and Steer alternate moves. Steer tries to reach either the **10 north** or **10 south** space, for if she arrives at either of those spaces, she gains freedom through the "Broken Fence". Rancher wins by landing on same space that Steer is on — or if Steer lands on same space that Rancher is on.

6 If neither Rancher nor Steer wins before all cards are used, children shuffle both decks and resume play. Game cannot end in a draw. Children also shuffle cards and resume play if remaining cards are "undesirable" (see below).

Example of remaining cards being "undesirable":
Steer is at **7 north**, Rancher at **5 north**. Thus both players want to move north. If all cards remaining are **red**, then they are all "undesirable". At such a juncture, children shuffle both decks and resume play.

CAMPFIRE CHAT

1 Who won more at your game: the Steer, or the Rancher? **A: Answers will vary, but game is designed so that the chances of winning are about 50-50.**

2 If you want to move north, from what deck should you draw cards?
A: From the black deck.

3 If you want to move south, from what deck should you draw cards?
A: From the red deck.

4 When you were the Steer, did you ever start out heading for one "Broken Fence", then turn around and head for the other "Broken Fence"? If so, why? **A: Steer should realize that if she is at first ahead of Rancher heading north or south, but then Rancher passes her in that direction, she is better off changing directions. That way she cannot accidentally run into Rancher on next turn. Example: On first move, Steer draws a black 2. Then Rancher draws a black 3. Playing smart, Steer should switch directions and draw a red card, for by doing so she can't accidentally run into Rancher.**

TIPS AND POINTERS

1 To let children play more and shuffle less, use cards from three decks when creating the black and red piles. With this set-up, black pile contains 6 black aces, 6 black 2s, 6 black 3s, and 2 black 4s. Red pile contains 6 red aces, 6 red 2s, 6 red 3s, and 2 red 4s.

2 Model game on an overhead or at a desk before children play. It's important to show them how to move their pieces.

ROUNDUP

FOR EACH PAIR OR GROUP OF PLAYERS:

➤ One pile with three red aces (i.e. any combination of hearts or diamonds), three red 2s, three red 3s, and one red 4.

➤ One pile with three black aces (i.e. any combination of spades or clubs), three black 2s, three black 3s, and one black 4.

➤ Note that you'll need cards from two decks to assemble these piles, but it's worth it!

➤ One Steer on the Loose! Card Layout Sheet from master on p.70 for every pair or group. Children may discard this sheet once they get a feel for the card layout.

➤ One Steer on the Loose! Gameboard from master on p.71 for every pair or group.

➤ Two tokens to move on the gameboard.

Steer on the Loose! Card Layout Sheet

DISCARD **RED** cards here. →

PICK UP **RED** cards to go **SOUTH (DOWN)** →

PICK UP **BLACK** cards to go **NORTH (UP)** →

DISCARD **BLACK** cards here. →

RED DISCARD PILE

RED PILE

BLACK PILE

BLACK DISCARD PILE

BROKEN FENCE = FREEDOM!!!

10 north	10 north
9 north	9 north
8 north	8 north
7 north	7 north
6 north	6 north
5 north	5 north
4 north	4 north
3 north	3 north
2 north	2 north
1 north	1 north
0	**0**
1 south	1 south
2 south	2 south
3 south	3 south
4 south	4 south
5 south	5 south
6 south	6 south
7 south	7 south
8 south	8 south
9 south	9 south
10 south	10 south

STEER

RANCHER

Steer on the Loose! Gameboard

BROKEN FENCE = FREEDOM!!!

CONCEPT CORRAL

NUMBER & OPERATION

➤ Learn how to add whole numbers.

➤ Develop and use strategies for whole number computation.

DATA ANALYSIS

➤ Gather data and draw conclusions based on it.

PROBABILITY

➤ Learn that probability is the likelihood that, given a range of possible events, a particular event will occur.

REASONING

➤ Figure out the probability that certain events will occur.

Cookie Thieves

GAME A Cooperative

GOAL: To add two numbers and record number sentences, and in the process, to catch the cookie thieves "red-handed".

 # Players: 2, 3, or 4.

1 Each group of children shuffles cards in their deck.

2 Children take two cards off top of the deck and place them face up.

3a If both cards are black, or if one is black and the other red, the thieves got away, and the sum of the two cards represents the number of cookies they stole.

3b But if both cards are red, the thieves have been caught "red-handed", and the sum of the two cards represents the number of cookies you caught them with, which will be returned to the other cowpokes.

4 The partners add up the amount on the two cards. You may want them to write the number sentence on Addition Worksheet A. They should write the sentence in black if the thieves got away, and write it in red if the thieves were caught "red-handed".

5 Have one child add up the number sentence while the other child records it, then let them switch roles. This way both children get practice adding and recording.

GAME B Cooperative

GOAL: To add three numbers and record the number sentences, and in the process, to catch the dastardly cookie thieves.

 # Players: 2, 3, or 4.

Same rules in Game A, except now children use three cards and add all three numbers together. They record their answers on Addition Worksheet B. In this game, children need all three cards to be red in order to catch the cookie thieves "red-handed".

 CAMPFIRE CHAT

1 What's the fewest cookies the thieves can steal on one turn in Game A? **A: 2 (two aces).**

2 What's the most cookies the thieves can steal on one turn in Game A? **A: 20 (two 10s). Note that answer will be less if children use a customized deck, as described in Tips & Pointers 1.**

3 In Game A, looking at how many of your answers are red and how many are black, what happens more often — that you catch the thieves "red-handed", or that they get away? **A: The thieves get away more often than they are caught.**

4 Why do you think the thieves get away more often than they are caught in Game A? **A: You cannot expect children to know this, but they can grasp the answer if you display it for all to see. The thieves get away more often than they are caught because there are four possibilities, only one of which results in the thieves being caught:.**

The possibilities are:

a) First card black, second card black, Thieves get away. Boo!

b) First card black, second card red. Thieves get away. Boo!

c) First card red, second card black. Thieves get away. Boo!

d) First card red, second card red. Thieves get CAUGHT. YAY!!!

So there is just one chance in four that the thieves get caught. All things being equal, they should get caught about one-quarter of the time.

5 What's the least number of cookies the thieves can steal on one turn in Game B? **A: 3 (three aces).**

6 What's the greatest number of cookies the thieves can steal on one turn in Game B? **A: 30 (three 10s). Note that answer will be less if children use a customized deck, as described in Tips & Pointers 2.**

7 In Game B, looking at how many of your answers are red and how many are black, what happens more often — that you catch the thieves "red-handed", or that they get away? **A: The thieves get away more often than they are caught.**

ROUNDUP

FOR EACH GROUP OF CHILDREN:

➥ **One deck with all picture cards and Jokers removed. The ace stands for the number 1. You can use all cards from 1 - 10 if your children can add to 20 (Game A) and to 30 (Game B). If not, you can customize the deck. (See Tips and Pointers 1 & 2.)**

➥ **Addition Worksheet A on p.94 to record number sentences in Game A, or Addition Worksheet B on p.95 to record number sentences in Game B.**

➥ **OPTIONAL: Treat Coupons copied from the master on p.75.**

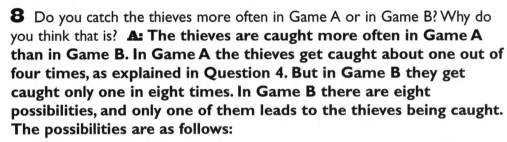

8 Do you catch the thieves more often in Game A or in Game B? Why do you think that is? **A: The thieves are caught more often in Game A than in Game B. In Game A the thieves get caught about one out of four times, as explained in Question 4. But in Game B they get caught only one in eight times. In Game B there are eight possibilities, and only one of them leads to the thieves being caught. The possibilities are as follows:**

a) First card black, second card black, third card black. Thieves get away. Boo!

b) First card black, second card black, third card red. Thieves get away. Boo!

c) First card black, second card red, third card black. Thieves get away. Boo!

d) First card black, second card red, third card red. Thieves get away. Boo!

e) First card red, second card black, third card black. Thieves get away. Boo!

f) First card red, second card black, third card red. Thieves get away. Boo!

g) First card red, second card red, third card black. Thieves get away. Boo!

h) First card red, second card red, third card red. Thieves get caught. All things being equal, the thieves should get caught only one-eighth of the time in Game B.

TIPS AND POINTERS

1 In deciding which cards to include in Game A deck, consider what number you want children to add to. Take half of that number, and use the cards from that number on down. Example: If you want children to add to 12, use all cards from ace through 6.

2 To decide which cards to include in Game B deck, consider what number you want children to add to. Take a third of that number, and use the cards from that number on down. Example: If you want children to add to 12, use all cards from ace through 4.

3 It often helps to let children use manipulative counters to add the numbers.

4 As children play, it's fun to congratulate them whenever they catch the thieves. You may want to give children redeemable treat coupons (copied off the master on p.75) for every five thieves they capture.

Treat Coupon Master

1   **1**

TREAT COUPON
FOR COURAGE IN CAPTURING
COOKIE THIEVES

1   **1**

TREAT COUPON
FOR COURAGE IN CAPTURING
COOKIE THIEVES

1   **1**

TREAT COUPON
FOR COURAGE IN CAPTURING
COOKIE THIEVES

1   **1**

TREAT COUPON
FOR COURAGE IN CAPTURING
COOKIE THIEVES

1   **1**

TREAT COUPON
FOR COURAGE IN CAPTURING
COOKIE THIEVES

1   **1**

TREAT COUPON
FOR COURAGE IN CAPTURING
COOKIE THIEVES

1   **1**

TREAT COUPON
FOR COURAGE IN CAPTURING
COOKIE THIEVES

1   **1**

TREAT COUPON
FOR COURAGE IN CAPTURING
COOKIE THIEVES

STORYLINE

There's a wild bull at this year's rodeo called "Nine-Second" Ned, so named because no cow rustler has ever ridden him for 10 seconds or more (though a few have held on for an amazing nine seconds). Young rodeo stars try to stay on Ned for the maximum of nine seconds, but not a second longer. If they do this enough times, they may just win the Rodeo Trophy.

CONCEPT CORRAL

NUMBER & OPERATION
➤ Count to nine and beyond.
➤ Add a string of whole numbers.

DATA ANALYSIS
➤ Figure out whether or not drawing a card might push a card total beyond nine.

PROBABILITY
➤ Study odds of getting a card that would be in a child's favor.

REASONING
➤ Determining how safe it is to take another card.

CONNECTIONS
➤ Discover links between addition and probability.

"Nine-Second" Ned

GAME A Cooperative

GOAL: Aspiring rodeo stars work together to collect enough tokens to win the Rodeo Trophy.

 # Players: 1, 2, 3, or 4.

1 Children shuffle deck and place it face down. They put 10 to 20 tokens in a bowl or container called "the pot". Children take four tokens from the pot and place these tokens on the table. Then children turn over the two cards on top of the deck.

2 Children add the two cards, and the sum represents the number of seconds they have stayed on Ned so far. i.e. If cards are 2 and 4, it means they have stayed on Ned for 6 seconds. Children discuss whether or not to take another card.

3 Consequences of card draws: a) If children draw a card, that makes their sum 8 or less, they take one token from the pot as a reward, since they have stayed on the wild bull. **b)** If they draw a card that makes their sum 9, they take two tokens from the pot, since they stayed on Ned for maximum possible time. **c)** But if card drawn makes sum 10 or more, Ned knocks them off, and they must return two of their tokens to the pot. (See p.78 for visual explanation.)

4 Children may draw as many cards as they wish or dare on any turn. Also, children don't have to take a card on any turn. But in some cases, they would lose out by not taking a card. i.e. If first two cards have a sum of 3, there's no way to get knocked off by taking a card, since highest card they can get is 4, and 3 + 4 is only 7.

5 Children try to win as many tokens as Educator specifies it takes to win Rodeo Star Trophy, which can be copied off the master on p.80. It's fun to start with a goal of 10 tokens, and gradually increase goal number as children become more comfortable with the game.

6 If children run out of tokens, they lose that rodeo match, but start another.

GOAL: Each rodeo star tries to collect the most tokens, or to be the only player with tokens left after all other players have run out. Whoever does so wins the Rodeo Trophy.

Players: 2, 3, or 4.

1 Shuffle and place deck face down. Put 10 tokens in the pot for every child playing. Each player takes four tokens from the pot. Child who is Dealer gives each player two cards face up.

2 Player to right of Dealer checks sum of his two cards. Player tells Dealer whether or not he wants another card (he may pass, if he wishes). If he takes a card and it makes his cards sum to eight or less, player takes one token from pot. If it makes his cards sum to nine, player takes two tokens from pot. But if it makes his cards sum to 10 or more, player must return two of his tokens to pot. Player may draw as many cards as he wants or dares to take. If a player runs out of tokens, he is out for the rest of that game.

3 Next player takes the same kind of turn as first player.

4 Two ways to win: **a)** be first player to collect 10 tokens, or **b)** become only player with tokens left after all other players have lost their tokens. Either way, winner gets Rodeo Trophy.

1 How did you decide whether or not to take another card?
A: Answers will vary, but children generally realize that it's safer to take a card if they have a lower sum, and riskier to take a card if they have a higher sum.

2 Did you ever know that it was completely safe to take another card? If so, how did you know? **A: Answers will vary, but some children will realize that any time their sum is 5 or less, there is no risk in taking a card. This is because the highest card they can get is a 4, and 5 + 4 = 9, and therefore they take no risk of getting thrown off of Ned.**

3 Did you ever decide it was too risky to take another card? If so, how did you know? **A: Answers will vary, but children often say that if you have a high sum — like a 7 or an 8 — it's risky to take another card.**

4 Did you ever feel so motivated to get a 9 that, even though you were close to 9, you drew a card? Did your risk pay off? **A: Answers will vary.**

5 Did your group ever get into an argument over whether or not to take another card? If so, how did you resolve the argument? **A: Answers will vary, but the ideas expressed will reveal children's understanding — or lack of understanding — of the addition and probability aspects of the game.**

ROUNDUP

FOR EACH CHILD OR GROUP OF CHILDREN:

➤ Deck with just the aces, 2s, 3s, and 4s. Add Jokers if you want children to see effect of adding 0.

➤ Small bowl or container to put tokens in. This bowl is referred to as "the pot".

➤ Game A: 10 to 20 tokens.

➤ Game B: 10 tokens for each child playing (e.g. 30 tokens for three players).

➤ OPTIONAL: Manipulative counters (buttons, beans, etc.) to help some children keep track of their totals.

➤ OPTIONAL: "Nine-Second" Ned Gameboard, from master on p.79. One for any child who needs it to keep track of his total. Each child using gameboard will need to place a token on the gameboard to keep track of his place.

➤ OPTIONAL: Rodeo Star Trophies copied off master on p.80, to be used as fun rewards.

77

1 It's best to play cooperative game first, so all get comfortable with rules.

2 If children have trouble adding a string of numbers in their head, let them use the "Nine-Second" Ned Gameboard on p.79. To use gameboard, children put a token on the sum of the first two cards. They advance token as many numbers as are indicated on card or cards drawn. Example: If first two cards are 2 and 3, token is placed on the sum, **5**. If next card is a 2, children move token two more places to **7**. This way they can see how close they are to falling off the wild bull.

3 In cooperative game, encourage children to confer when deciding whether or not to draw another card. Also encourage them to remember what they talk about during conferences, so they can share their ideas during the Campfire Chat.

4 Consider using cards from two or more decks so children play more and shuffle less.

5 If you wish to emphasize games's probability aspects, ask children questions as they play. Helpful questions include: **a)** Given the sum you have, are there any cards that would be safe to get? **b)** Are there any cards that could knock you off of Ned? **c)** Of the four kinds of cards in the deck (aces, 2s, 3s and 4s), how many would be safe to get? How many would knock you off the bull? **d)** Given this breakdown of safe to unsafe cards, do you think it's safe or risky to draw a card? And why?

6 You might suggest that children use a special layout to arrange the tokens they collect. For example: Arrange tokens in rows of 2 to learn to count by 2s; in rows of 5 to learn to count by 5s.

"Nine-Second" Ned Overview

Sum of 8 or less ... take 1 token.

Sum of 9 ... take 2 tokens!

Sum of 10 or more ... put 2 tokens back! Ouch!

"Nine-Second" Ned Gameboard

1	2	3	4	5	6	7	8	9	10 or more

Off to a good start!

Hang in there!

Don't let go!

Hang onto that bull!

Going strong!

You can do it!

Hang on tight!

Keep going ...

GREAT RIDE!

BYE, BYE! YOU'RE IN THE AIR!

Rodeo Trophy Master

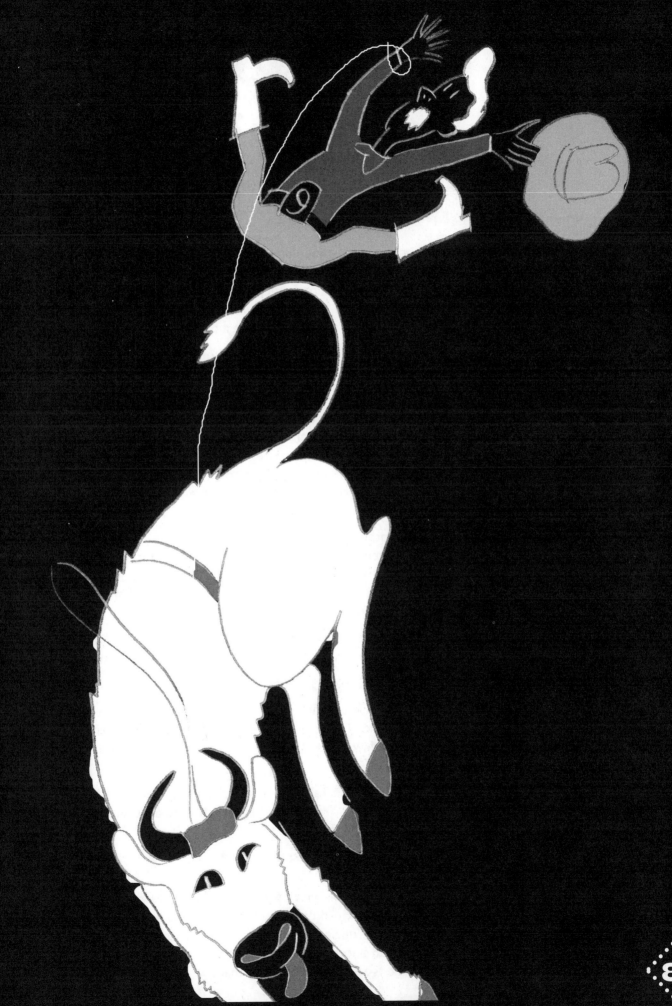

CONCEPT CORRAL

NUMBER & OPERATION
➥ Learn to "add on": the skill of adding a number to another number, or to a previously calculated sum.
➥ Gain fluency with addition facts.

PROBABILITY
➥ Gain introductory grasp of probability by exploring probability of certain outcomes (described in Campfire Chat questions).

REASONING
➥ Distinguish between games of luck and games of skill.

Pre-req skill: basic addition.

Pony Express

GAME A Cooperative

GOAL: To move the Pony Express horse-token from start to finish — from 0 to 10.

 # Players: 1, 2, or 3.

1 Each child or group gets one Pony Express Gamesheet. Depending on how many children are in a group, children assign themselves one or more roles. Commonly used roles are: Dealer (shuffles and turns over cards), Rider (advances the token), and Scribe (writes numbers on gamesheet). Children may rotate roles round-robin style after each game.

2 Children place a token (buttons work well) on 0 space of gamesheet's number line (the "Station 1" space). Dealer shuffles and places deck face down.

3 Dealer turns first card over. Rider advances horse-token number of spaces on card. i.e. If card is a 3, Rider moves token from 0 to 3. Then Scribe fills in first number sentence with the correct numbers (in this example: **0 + 3 = 3**). Scribe also writes the 3 in box that begins next number sentence. Tell children the gray arrows and same-shape recording spaces (square, triangle, circle, etc.) remind Scribe to rewrite sum at start of next line.

4 Dealer lays another card face up on top of first upturned card. Rider advances horse-token that many spaces. i.e. If new card is a 2, Rider advances horse-token 2 more spaces, so it lands on 5. Scribe completes second number sentence (in this case, it would read: **3 + 2 = 5**). Scribe also writes 5 in first space of next number sentence.

5 If card drawn makes sum exceed 10, card is discarded. i.e. If token is on 8 and Dealer draws a 4, this 4 is discarded, and Dealer draws another card.

6 Play continues until token reaches 10 exactly.

7 It's fun for children keep track of how many cards it took them to reach goal-number each time. They can compete against themselves, trying to reach goal-number with as few turns as possible, or with as many turns as possible.

GAME B Competitive

GOAL: To move the Pony Express horse-token from start to finish more quickly than any other rider.

 # Players: 2, 3, or 4.

Rules: Same as Game A, with a few exceptions. In this game, each child gets her own gamesheet. Children draw from same deck, but each child draws a card for herself, one at a time. As each card is turned over, child who turned it over advances her token that many spaces. Whoever's horse-token reaches goal number first wins that round.

CAMPFIRE CHAT

1 How can you tell if it's possible to win with just one more card? **A: If goal number is 10, and if you are at 6 or higher, it's possible to win with one more card, since you can get a 4, 3, 2, or 1.**

2 How can you tell if it's not possible to win with just one more card? **A: If goal number is 10, and if you are at 5 or lower, it's not possible to win with one more card, for the highest card you can get is a 4, and 5 + 4 falls short of 10.**

3 What's the greatest number of cards it can take to get to 10? **A: Seven cards (four aces and three 2s). Note: the law of probability shows that this should happen just once every 16,000 times that you play. That's why we didn't bother to put a seventh line on the sheet. If this does happen, celebrate!**

4 What's the least number of cards it can take to get to 10? **A: Three (either two 4s and a 2, or one 4 and two 3s). Note: the probability that either of these will happen are about 8 out of 100. In other words, play the game enough, and you should see this happen.**

5 Can you find a way to use the idea of "adding on" that this game teaches. In other words, if you have a problem like 2 + 3 + 4, can you use "adding on" to solve it? **A: Yes, first find the sum of 2 and 3, then add 4 to that sum.**

6 Is any skill involved in either the cooperative or competitive game? Or was this all luck? In other words, did you make choices that could help you or hurt you? **A: No skill is involved, only luck, for children do not make any choices that can help or hurt them.**

ROUNDUP

FOR EACH CHILD OR GROUP OF CHILDREN:

➤ All four aces, 2s, 3s, and 4s. Ace stands for 1. Don't use Joker in this game.

➤ Pony Express Gamesheet, copied off master on p.84. One per group for Game A; one per child for Game B.

TIPS AND POINTERS

1 While gamesheet on p.84 is designed so children make sums adding to 10 (the goal number), you can modify gamesheet if you wish to change the goal number. For young children, you may want to specify a smaller goal number, perhaps 5. To help children see that 5 is their goal number, have them circle the 5 on the number line. Deck in this case would contain just aces and 2s. More experienced counters, on the other hand, might draw a number line from 0 through 20 on a separate sheet of paper and use that. In this case, deck would use all cards from ace through 6.

2 Model how to play before letting children play. It's fun to play as a large group first, letting all children keep track on their own gamesheets. Then you can monitor to see if all children understand how to move tokens and record number sentences.

3 Emphasize that children COUNT MOVES, NOT SPACES. i.e. If horse-token is on 2 and child draws 3, she counts one for MOVING from 2 to 3, another for MOVING from 3 to 4, and the final one for MOVING from 4 to 5. Using horse motif, tell children they count every time horse GALLOPS.

4 You may want to copy gamesheet onto both sides of a piece of paper so children can play four games with one sheet.

5 To help children see how this game relates to addition, you might ask them to write down the addition number sentence that adds up to the goal number. i.e. If cards used are 2, 1, 4, and 3, children would write the number sentence: 2 + 1 + 4 + 3 = 10. They can do this on a separate sheet of paper.

6 It's fun to share the history of the Pony Express (sidebar of p.85).

Pony Express Gamesheet

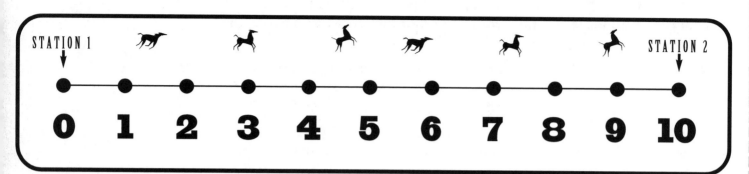

0 1 2 3 4 5 6 7 8 9 10

Game 1

0 + ___ = ▢

▢ + ___ = △

△ + ___ = ○

○ + ___ = ⬠

⬠ + ___ = ⏢

⏢ + ___ = ◇

Game 2

0 + ___ = ▢

▢ + ___ = △

△ + ___ = ○

○ + ___ = ⬠

⬠ + ___ = ⏢

⏢ + ___ = ◇

HISTORY CONNECTION
The Story of the Pony Express

Today the mail travels by airplane, truck, and mailvan. But for a time in the old West, mail was carried by man and horse. This system was called the Pony Express.

The Pony Express delivered mail from St. Joseph, Missouri, all the way to San Francisco, California (and back again), a one-way journey of 1,800 miles.

Riders would ride from one station to another, and there were 157 stations in all. To keep the mail moving quickly, riders would switch horses as often as six to eight times between stations.

The Pony Express was remarkably fast for its time, for it was able to deliver the mail a distance of 1,800 miles in 10 days. That's an average of 180 miles a day!

Note that every pair of stations was approximately 1,800/156 miles apart, which is approximately 11 miles apart. You can therefore tell children that each space on the Gameboard represents about one mile.

"Monster" Rattlesnakes

STORYLINE

Daring buckaroos comb the prairie for huge rattlers. They pick cards from the deck that tell them how big to make their rattlesnakes. They can play cooperatively to form one huge, "monster" rattlesnake, or compete to make the longest rattler.

CONCEPT CORRAL

NUMBER & OPERATION
➤ Use addition to form rattlesnakes.

MEASUREMENT
➤ Compare lengths using various non-standard units (paperclips, plastic links, paper links). In this game write-up, all of these are referred to generically as "links".

REASONING
➤ Predict how changing size of link affects length of snakes. Then create new snakes to test predictions.

REPRESENTATION
➤ Draw depictions of rattlesnakes to show the correct number of links or paper clips.

GAME A Cooperative

GOAL: Buckaroos work together to make the longest rattlesnake possible.

 # Players: 2, 3, or 4.

1 Each child takes a turn picking a card off top of deck and collecting that number of **medium-sized links** to begin creating his section of "monster" rattlesnake.

2 On each new turn, each child adds as many links to his section of snake as indicated by card drawn. Example: If a child draws a 3 on first turn, a 6 on second turn, and a 7 on third turn, his section of snake would be **3 + 6 + 7 = 16** units long after his third turn. (Children can record this sentence on Addition Worksheet B on p.95, if desired.) Educator's discretion as to how many turns are allowed. Two is a good starting number. Once children get the idea, they may want to take more turns.

3 Each child then draws a picture of his own snake.

4 Once all snakes have been assembled, children in each group put snakes together to create "monster" rattlesnake.

5 Once "monster" rattlesnake is created, children count how many links long the snake is. Educator may need to assist with this step. This fact can also be recorded at bottom of Addition Worksheet B on p.95.

6 Children may enjoy creating a "monster" rattlesnake in this way: **a)** first each child cuts out his own drawing of his snake, **b)** then all children put their drawings together to assemble the "monster" snake.

GAME B Competitive

GOAL: Every cowpoke tries to make a rattlesnake longer than the other cowpoke's rattlesnakes.

 # Players: 2, 3, or 4.

Same rules as in Game A, except now the children do not combine their snakes at the end, and each child wants his snake to be the longest. Educator's discretion as to how many cards each child may draw before snake is considered complete.

GOAL: Buckaroos predict whether or not changing length of link will change length of snake. Then they test their predictions.

 # Players: 2, 3, or 4.

1 Each group of children makes a "monster" rattlesnake using the **medium-sized links** — as in Game A.

2 Children lay snake on the floor so that it lies perfectly straight.

3 Educator shows children **small links**, and asks them to imagine making a snake with them. Educator asks them to imagine using the same number of **small links** as they used to make their "monster" rattlesnake in Step 1.

4 Children predict whether such a snake made with the **small links** would be longer, shorter, or same length as the "monster" rattlesnake made in Step 1. Educator may want to record predictions, group by group.

5 Children make a second snake using same number of **small links** as the number of **medium-sized links** used in Step 1. Then children lay both "monster" rattlesnakes side by side and straight to compare lengths. Children discuss how the results either do or don't match their predictions.

6 Repeat steps 2 - 4 using the **large links**.

7 Have children create a mini-snake with just five links of each type: **small**, **medium**, and **large**. Ask them to draw these three mini-snakes on a sheet of paper. Ask them to circle the picture of the longest mini-snake.

CAMPFIRE CHAT

1 Do you always get a longer snake if you draw more cards, and a shorter snake if you draw fewer cards? **A: This may be true in general, but it is not necessarily true. Example: It's possible that in five draws, you could get 1 + 3 + 1 + 2 + 2 = just 9 links, while in just two draws you could get 10 + 10 = 20 links!**

2 Did any group predict that all three snakes in Game C would be the same length? What did you learn when you made all three snakes in Game C? **A: Children should learn that the length of the link does affect the length of the snake.**

3 How does the length of the link affect the length of the snake? **A: If number of total links per snake remains the same, the longer the link, the longer the snake. And vice-versa: the**

ROUNDUP

FOR EACH GROUP OF CHILDREN:

➤ **One deck of all numbered cards from ace through 10.**

➤ **Paper on which children draw their snakes.**

➤ **Standard small paper clips (1 1/4" long), which serve as the small links.**

➤ **Standard plastic links (1 11/16" long), which serve as the medium-sized links.**

➤ **Standard large paper clips (1 7/8" long), which serve as the large links.**

➤ **OPTIONAL: Jumbo paper clips, which can be found at office supply stores. (If you use jumbo links, they become the large links, large paper clips become the medium-sized links, and small paper clips are the small links. With such a set-up, don't use plastic links.)**

➤ **OPTIONAL: Addition Worksheet B on p.95 for children to record addition sentences.**

➤ **NOTE: In this write-up, both paper clips and plastic links are referred to as "links".**

87

shorter the link, the shorter the snake.

4 Suppose that instead of using links, you lay together units that don't link, such as shoes or pencils. In that case, can you think of a unit that would make a snake longer than your longest snake, or shorter than your shortest snake? **A: Answers will vary, but answers will show whether or not children understand the concept of size. For the longer snake, children should choose a unit longer than their longer snake's unit. e.g. A ruler, piece of paper, the length of a desk. For the shorter snake, children should choose a unit that is shorter than their shorter snake's unit. e.g. A dime, a button, width of a pencil eraser, etc.**

Extension: Based on the answers generated by question 4, promote a group discussion on what kinds of objects make better measuring units than others. Example: if children suggest a shoe in question 4, you might ask them if all shoes are the same size. And if not, then would that make a good unit or not? And what might make a better unit? This can segue into a discussion on the need for standardized units of length: the inch, centimeter, etc.

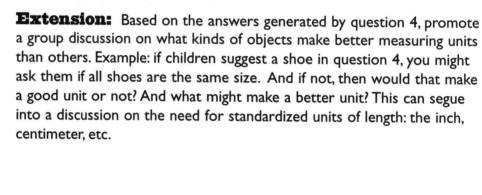

TIPS AND POINTERS

1 This game offers children an introduction to concept of length.

2 You may want children to use Addition Worksheet B on p.95 to record their addition sentences.

3 Show children that when they draw snakes, they shouldn't try to draw them in a straight line because if they do so, they may not fit on their drawing page. Show them how to draw a snake with curves so that it does fit on drawing page.

Extension: Use links to measure and record lengths of other objects, or to measure heights of the children themselves!

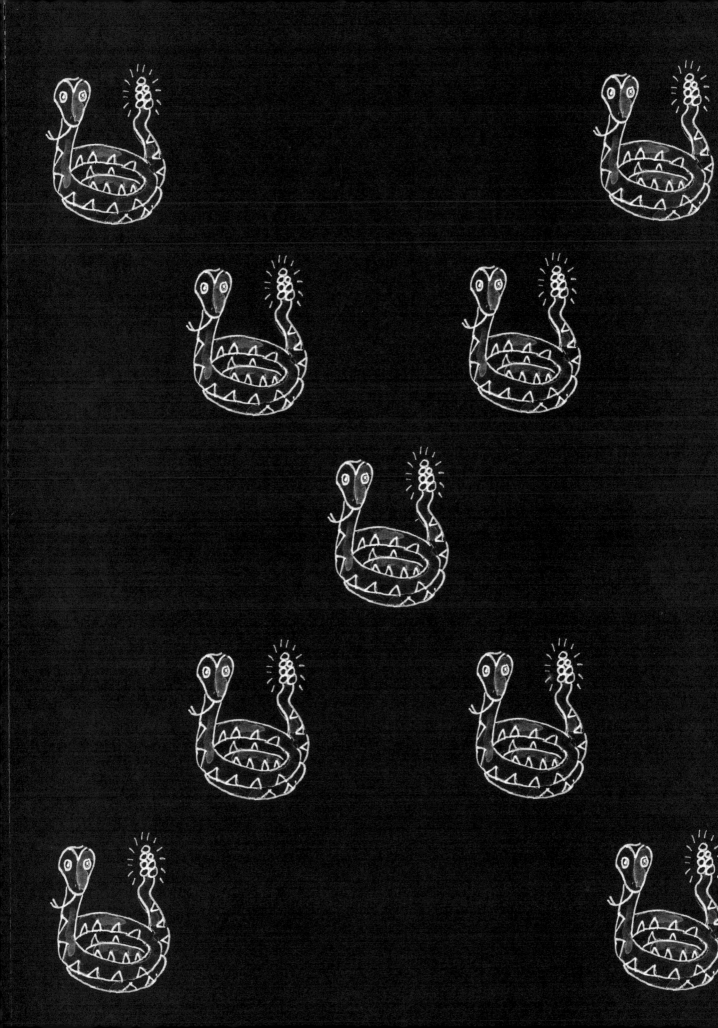

Counting Sheep

After spending an afternoon rustling steer, the cowpokes are so excited that they can't sit still. This game helps them settle down — and also teaches them about the passage of time. (A great game to play after active play, when children need to calm down and re-focus.)

CONCEPT CORRAL

NUMBER & OPERATION
➤ Estimate how much time has elapsed during a quiet time.

MEASUREMENT
➤ Develop a sense of duration of one minute, two minutes, three minutes, four minutes, and five minutes.

REASONING
➤ Distinguish concepts of "greater than" and "less than".

GAME A Cooperative

GOAL: To try to be quiet for a specified time period.

 # Players: 1 or more.

1 Shuffle deck and place it on table. Select one child to be the Card Chooser, and another to be the Timer.

2 Card Chooser takes top card off the deck, and shows it to the class. This number tells how many minutes can be earned.

3 The Timer gives a starting signal and starts keeping track of time. Timer's job is to monitor the amount of time elapsed and to let everyone know when each minute elapses. You may, for example, want Timer to make a tally mark on board to show that one minute has passed, two minutes, etc.

4 When time is up or someone speaks or laughs, Timer stops the time, and the number of minutes that children stayed quiet is recorded as the score.

GAME B Cooperative

GOAL: To be quiet for a certain time period, then estimate if it was for more or less than a certain number of minutes.

 # Players: 1 or more.

1 Educator draws top card off the deck, but does not reveal card to children.

2 If card is black, Educator asks children to stay quiet for a time period just over one minute. If card is red, Educator asks them to stay quiet for a time period just less than one minute.

3 Educator tells children when to start being quiet, and when they can talk again. Before they start being quiet, children put heads down so they cannot glance at a clock or watch.

4 Once time is up and children can talk, Educator has them to vote on whether they think they were quiet for more than a minute or less than a minute.

5 After the vote, Educator reveals the card, and children find out if their guess was right or wrong.

Game B Suggestion: When first playing, it helps to make time period 10 - 15 seconds more than a minute for black cards and 10 - 15 seconds less than a minute for red cards. That gives children a fair chance — but not too easy a chance — to estimate duration of elapsed time. As children get better at this game, make the time closer to the minute on either side, say 5 - 10 seconds more, or 5 - 10 seconds less than the minute, to make game more fun and challenging.

GOAL: To be quiet for a certain time period, then estimate how long it was for.

 # Players: 1 or more.

Same basic play as Game B, with a few differences.

1 Deck is just aces and 2s, to start out.

2 Black suits still mean Educator goes over the minute, and red suits still mean Educator goes under the minute. But now the number on the card is significant too, for it tells how many minutes it's all in relation to. Examples: Red ace means children stay quiet for less than one minute; black ace means children stay quiet for more than one minute; red 2 means children stay quiet for less than two minutes; black 2 means children stay quiet for more than two minutes.

Game C Suggestion: A good rule when starting out is to add or subtract about 20 seconds. i.e. Red 2 means have children be quiet for 1:40; black 2 means have them be quiet for 2:20. As children get better at estimating duration of time elapsed, add or subtract less time to make time closer to the actual minute. This allows you to make the game gradually more challenging.

Extension: As children get better at estimating passage of time, add the 3s, then the 4s, finally the 5s to the deck, and see how well children can estimate times like: less than 3 minutes, more than 4 minutes, etc.

ROUNDUP

FOR EACH CHILD OR GROUP OF CHILDREN:

➤ Games A and B: Deck with just the aces, 2s, 3s, 4s, and 5s.

➤ Game C: deck with just the aces and 2s, but you slowly can add more cards to deck.

➤ A clock, watch, or stopwatch.

➤ A system to keep track of how many minutes the children are able to keep quiet. i.e. Graph, marble jar, number line, etc.

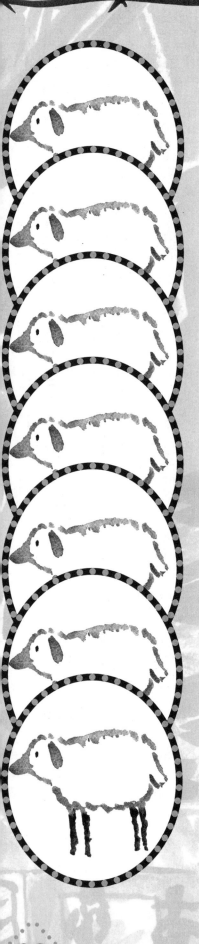

1 Was it harder than you thought — or easier than you thought — to keep quiet for the time specified in Game A? Why? **A: Answers will vary.**

2 In Game B, did you tend to overestimate or underestimate the length of time? And why do you think that was? **A: Answers will vary.**

3 As you played Game B more and more, did you eventually become better at figuring out how much time had gone by? **A: Answers will vary.**

4 As you played Games B and C, what strategies did you use to figure out how long it took? Did you use any strategies that didn't work? What were the best strategies? **A: Answers will vary.**

5 In which game did you find it easiest to be quiet? Game A, Game B, or Game C? Why? **A: Answers will vary, but often children say they find it easier to be quiet in Games B and C because their minds were busy with the time-estimation challenge.**

6 In which game did it seem like the time passed most quickly? Why do you think that is? **A: Answers will vary.**

7 Is there any difference between "more than a minute" and "less than two minutes", or do they mean the same thing? Explain. **A: Answers will vary.**

TIPS AND POINTERS

1 Game A: It's fun to set a goal for the children to meet, as in: "We can be quiet for 5 minutes total, and then plan a reward." Depending how often you play this game you may want to set a goal that children have to work for.

2 Game A: If children do make a noise before the goal time is achieved, they can still earn credit for the time they were quiet. The bigger the number drawn from the deck, the more points children can earn.

3 Game A: It helps to have the child who is the Timer mark on the board or hold up a finger to help the other children keep track of the time passing.

How to Make a Simple, Effective Card Holder

Method A — (Easier, but less secure)

MATERIALS NEEDED:

➡ Two lids from cottage cheese, sour cream, or butter tubs.

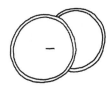

➡ One brad.

DIRECTIONS:

1. Poke a hole with a long-arm hole puncher or a sharp scissor in the center of each lid.

2. Place the covers back to back, so they are directly against each other and connect with the brad.

TO USE: Have children stick the cards between the two lids and hold onto the lids with their hands.

- -

Method B — (Bit harder, but more secure)

MATERIALS NEEDED:

➡ Two lids from cottage cheese, sour cream, or butter tubs.

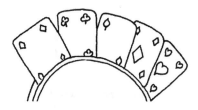

➡ Two buttons.

➡ One piece of pipe cleaner.

DIRECTIONS:

1. Make two small holes in the center of each lid.
2. Place the covers back to back, so they are directly against each other.
3. Place a 1/2"-3/4" button over the two holes, one on each side.
4. Use the pipe cleaner to connect the buttons and lids together.
5. Twist the pipe cleaner and cut off the extra.

TO USE: Have children stick the cards between the two lids and hold onto the lids with their hands.

Side view ➡

Addition Worksheet A

$$\square$$

$$=$$

$$\square$$

$$+$$

$$\square$$

$$\square$$

$$=$$

$$\square$$

$$+$$

$$\square$$

$$\square$$

$$=$$

$$\square$$

$$+$$

$$\square$$

$$\square$$

$$=$$

$$\square$$

$$+$$

$$\square$$

$$\square$$

$$=$$

$$\square$$

$$+$$

$$\square$$

$$\square$$

$$=$$

$$\square$$

$$+$$

$$\square$$

$$\square$$

$$=$$

$$\square$$

$$+$$

$$\square$$

$$\square$$

$$=$$

$$\square$$

$$+$$

$$\square$$

94

Addition Worksheet B

$=$ [ ]

$=$ [ ]

$=$ [ ]

$=$ [ ]

$=$ [ ]

$=$ [ ]

$=$ [ ]

$=$ [ ]

GAME	PAGES	REPRESENTATION	CONNECTIONS	COMMUNICATION	REASONING & PROOF	PROBLEM SOLVING	DATA & PROBABILITY	MEASUREMENT	GEOMETRY	ALGEBRA & PATTERNS	NUMBER & OPERATION
Racing Rattlers	6-9	✓		✓	✓					✓	✓
"Hungry" Hank	10-13				✓					✓	✓
Annie Oakley	14-19	✓	✓	✓	✓		✓				✓
"Howdy Do?"	20-23	✓	✓	✓	✓					✓	✓
"One-Two-Three-Draw!"	24-27		✓	✓	✓		✓				✓
Tail-Eating Snakes	28-33			✓	✓				✓		✓
Cloud Dreamin'	34-39	✓	✓	✓	✓				✓		
Galloping Guesses	40-43	✓		✓	✓		✓				
Hunting for Grub	44-49	✓	✓	✓	✓						✓
Stuck in the Mud	50-53			✓	✓					✓	✓
Mysterious Bandit	54-61	✓	✓	✓	✓	✓				✓	✓
"Howdy Pardner!"	62-67		✓	✓	✓	✓				✓	✓
Steer on the Loose!	68-71		✓	✓	✓	✓				✓	✓
Cookie Thieves	72-75			✓	✓		✓				✓
"Nine-Second" Ned	76-81		✓	✓	✓		✓				✓
Pony Express	82-85		✓	✓	✓		✓				✓
"Monster" Rattlesnakes	86-89	✓		✓	✓			✓			✓
Counting Sheep	90-92			✓	✓			✓			✓